RETURN OF THE WARRIORS

THÉUN MARES

ABOUT THE AUTHOR

The name Théun Mares, (pronounced Tayoon Mah-rez), is the closest rendering in the English language of the author's ancient Toltec name. It means "Théun of the Great Water".

Théun's function amongst Toltecs is what is known as the nagal* (pronounced nah-hal), or spiritual leader within a unit of warriors.

Born in Zimbabwe, of a father who was a gold miner, and a mother who was a natural seer, Théun spent most of his early life in the bush, amongst the animals, the birds and the natives of the area, with their rich and abundant folklore. It was in the wilds that Théun resumed his training in this current lifetime, under the tutelage of the Nagal J.

After studying for an Arts Degree at the University of Cape Town, Théun spent most of his working life in education.

During a year's study leave through Europe and North America in 1977, Théun began having flashbacks of his training as a warrior in previous lifetimes and, by 1978, his memory of all his previous training had been restored.

In 1992 Théun resigned from his work and started to prepare for his life as a nagal. In 1994 he started training the members of his unit, and also commenced his assignment of disclosing the Toltec teachings to the world at large through a series of books.

In addition to his own personal apprentices, Théun also has other people working under his guidance towards the furtherance of the evolution of awareness through the medium of the Toltec Tradition. He resides in Cape Town.

RETURN OF THE WARRIORS

THÉUN MARES

THE TOLTEC TEACHINGS

Volume One

lionheart
PUBLISHING

ISBN 1-919792-08-2 (Paperback)
ISBN 1-919792-09-0 (Hardcover)

Cover: The mosaic floor of the Toltec Temple showing the Sacred Centre, the Yellow Rose of Friendship, and the electromagnetic force fields generated by the temple.

Fronticepiece by Rochelle Beresford
Text Illustrations by Susan Emily
Cover and Interior design by Lori Gie

Printed and bound by National Book Printers
Drukkery Street, Goodwood, Western Cape

TM

This logo signifies that this work concerns the Toltec Path of Freedom as expressed by Théun Mares, and serves to differentiate these teachings from Meso-American traditions of Toltequity, Nagualism and Shamanism.

lionheart
PUBLISHING
Private Bag X5
Constantia, 7848
Cape Town
Republic of South Africa
e-mail: cajmi@iafrica.com
www.lionheartpublishing.com

This book is a salutation to my own beloved teacher, the Nagal J., who has always guided my fellow warriors and myself with the iron will and uncompromising discipline of a man who does not take his responsibility lightly, and yet his unconditional love for us all, and his profound wisdom, have ever been our deepest inspiration.

MAN

(Showing the luminous cocoon)

Magical being of the universe - that point at which perception is assembled.
(Monoprint: Rochelle Beresford)

CONTENTS

LIST OF ILLUSTRATIONS

ACKNOWLEDGEMENTS

To all the many people who have given so freely of their time and energy in helping me to bring these books into the light of day. A great big hug and thank-you to you all!

In a time even before time, when the orange-red sun was still young and the planet Earth was not yet born to flesh; when the heavens were still being torn asunder by the War of Spirit, and when man was as yet enveloped within the fiery mists of solar beingness ....

INTRODUCTION

Up until 1968 when Carlos Castaneda published his first book entitled *The Teachings of Don Juan: A Yaqui Way of Knowledge*, it was generally assumed that the Toltec tradition was long gone and forgotten. However, the curiosity and fascination sparked off by this book quickly earned for Mr. Castaneda not only fame and recognition, but also a large enthusiastic following, dotted here and there with the inevitable critics trying their level best to discredit him. Doing what he could to avoid the onslaughts of both fan and critic, Mr. Castaneda continued to bring out book after book in a quietly consistent manner. Now, many years later and after the publication of several books, the readers of Carlos Castaneda are still perplexed by two haunting questions – questions which neither his fans nor his critics have ever been able to answer with any great deal of satisfaction or conviction: firstly, did the now-legendary Don Juan really exist; and secondly, if Don Juan did exist, were Mr. Castaneda's incredible experiences real or fictional?

Although the nature of this book will make it appear at times as if it is an attempt to defend the personal claims of Carlos Castaneda, this is not the intention, for should Mr. Castaneda wish to be defended then he is assuredly very capable of doing so himself. This book has instead another purpose which is fourfold: firstly, to verify the continued existence of Toltecs throughout the ages; secondly, to substantiate the authenticity of the teachings to which Mr. Castaneda bears witness; thirdly, to reveal to the world at large the true essence of these ancient teachings; and fourthly, to pave the way for Toltec warriors as they return to the public eye after their long voluntary 'exile' to take their rightful place once again amongst the true spiritual leaders of mankind.

One point only will be made in defence of Carlos Castaneda, and this is that he could not have published what has heretofore always been a strictly oral tradition without the consent of the Toltecs. If the truth be told, Mr. Castaneda was destined to re-introduce to the world a system of knowledge which has for ages been assumed obsolete. The reason for this, and why this book reveals who the Toltecs are and what their tradition entails, is because the great wheel of evolution has turned a mighty circle. In response, the call has gone forth to Toltecs the world over to unite once again under the banner of their common goal, and to put their combined knowledge and power at the disposal of Those who have ever guided the destiny of all life upon this planet from behind the scenes – Those known to Toltecs as the Guardians of the Race. This call has gone forth because the world in general, and humanity in particular, has reached a crucial crossroad – a juncture which poses for all life upon this planet a vital choice, and at the same time an unprecedented opportunity.

This crossroad in the history of mankind, recorded in a prophecy of unimaginable antiquity, has long been in the planning and patiently awaited by the Guardians of the Race. As time has spun out the web of destiny Toltecs have come to recognise the part assigned to them in the history of the planet, and as their knowledge has grown they have begun to grasp this ancient prophecy for themselves. Here follows a transcript of this prophecy:

> 'Together we now will manifest the Temple of the Spirit!' cried the seventh Son, the Dragon. Thus the seven great Sons of Beingness, who are the enthroned Three, moved four-square to their places in the East, the North, the West and the South to commence their mighty task.
> The doors of the Temple were barred and guarded. Inside it

was dark for not yet could the Light shine forth. Thus was no part of the Temple visible. Not a sound disturbed the utter silence, for the sacred Word too could not yet be sounded. The Seven showed not their colour nor resonated their vibration, only a silent communication passed between them marking the progress of the work.

Aeons passed until at last there came the sounds of life from outside the Temple and a lesser son of Spirit knocked upon the Temple door. Briefly the Temple doors were opened to admit this son of man, and as he entered into the Temple so he too added his power to that which was within. So came the sons of earth one by one, and as they in turn were admitted into the Temple, so the light within began to flare ever brighter.

The sons of men traversed the Temple from North to South and from West to East. In the centre they came to stand before the Rose, and there they found the heart, the knowledge and the power to work. They pushed aside the veil to the inner shrine and stood bathed in pure White Light.

Time continued to pass, in which the Temple became ever more beautiful, as slowly its architecture, proportions, detail and finishes took form in the growing light.

Then came forth a call from the East: 'Open now the doors to all the sons of earth, so that they may seek the Light and find the Temple of the Spirit. Remove the veil to the inner shrine so that all may enter into Light. Let the Warriors of the Spirit, who have for so long concealed their labours, now precipitate upon the plains of earth the Temple of Life. Let the Light shine forth, let the Word too sound forth, let the work of transmutation begin.

'Thus it is that the Temple of Light shall be transferred to earth, to illumine there the dream of the dreamer. Thus will man awaken in the East, and by confronting his fear meet his challenges in the West. Thus shall man be guided to find respect in the South and gather his strength in the North. Then shall man seek the only true light and learn the secret of the orange-red Light which shines ever in the East.'

'Why are we to allow all this?' demand the Seven, the enthroned Three.

'For now the time has come, the Warriors are ready, and the Spirit has already moved in the light, so revealing the sacred colour and sounding the creative vibration. Now all the sons of men are able to seek power and to engage in the battle for freedom. Naught else remains to be done.'

'Then so be it,' answer the Seven, the enthroned Three. 'So will all the sons of earth go forth to do battle.'

So speaks the ancient prophecy, recorded in a time before time, from an oracle not of this world. The works of Carlos Castaneda, as well as this book, are but the fulfilment of this prophecy, for clearly the Toltec teachings belong to no one particular sect, but are the divine birthright of every man and woman.

Since the principal raison d'être of this and subsequent books is to put the reader in touch with the true essence of the Toltec teachings these books have, for the sake of clarity, been divided into separate volumes. Furthermore, so as to enable the reader to become systematically familiarised with this ancient teaching this first volume has been written in three parts. Starting from a broad overview each part gradually yields to greater detail and complexity.

The first part of this book covers the origin and historical development of the Toltec tradition. This history should be seen as the necessary backdrop against which to project the various concepts, since many of these will at first glance appear somewhat foreign.

The second part deals in depth with the fundamental concepts which form the framework of the teachings. These fundamentals must be grasped fully if the finer aspects of the teachings are to have any value at all.

Inherent within all of the Toltec teachings are a great many axiomatic expressions which are upheld as being the life-essence of the teachings. These axioms, which have traditionally been termed *aphorisms*, are universal and timeless truths. For ease of reference all the aphorisms used throughout this book have been lifted out of the text.

The third part of this volume contains detailed instructions on the first steps taken by all apprentices of the Toltec tradition. However, a word of caution is appropriate at this point, namely that the Warrior's Path* is like no other path known to man. As such it should not be rushed into helter-skelter, but approached with due consideration and respect.

In this day and age when the public is being offered all manner of ways in which to achieve so-called instant enlightenment, it will perhaps come as a disappointment to some to find that I am not claiming to bring the reader a formula for 'The Lazy Man's Way To Miracles'. I am not hereby implying that Toltecs are incapable of performing miracles, but merely that in order to do so even Toltecs have to serve a long and difficult apprenticeship. A condensed workshop yields a short-lived career and, as is well known, a little knowledge is inevitably dangerous knowledge.

I would be doing the reader an injustice if I were to infer that the Warrior's Path is easy, for this is far from the truth. Of all possible paths the Warrior's Path is quite honestly the most difficult. Few are the people who are prepared for the hardship required to obtain that knowledge which is needed in order to master the highest grades of this noble path. Nevertheless,

---

** The traditional name given to the Toltec teachings.*

provided that this path is tackled one step at a time, it is within every adult's capability to master enough of the elementary work to enhance the quality of his or her life beyond imagination.

The Warrior's Path is a bit like having to scale a sheer cliff face – at first glance it seems impossible, but then we see a handgrip, a foothold and we begin to climb, only to find more grips, more footholds. But the golden rule in such a climb is never to look up except to find another grip, and never to look down, to avoid being overcome by fear of failure.

It is a long haul to the top of the cliff, but what an accomplishment, what a freedom and what a *power*, and it all starts with the very simplest of exercises. Yet this is exactly where every apprentice discovers the first difficulty; namely that it all looks too easy and too simple. It is a Toltec axiom that everything which has *power* rarely, if ever, attracts attention, for man's rational mind is geared towards academic complexity.

Here lies the difficulty of the Warrior's Path, not in its academic complexity, but paradoxically, in its utter simplicity. Many of the teachings are so subtle as to be quickly and easily overlooked by the overly enthusiastic novice. Perhaps this point will be more firmly grasped if it is pointed out that in having read this far the reader has already taken his first step upon the Warrior's Path.

Apropos the origin and historical development of the Toltec tradition, the only comprehensively written documentation upon the Toltecs is the history of the Toltec civilization which flourished in the Valley of Mexico from 950 to 1160 C.E.* Yet this period is but a tiny part of the Toltecs' history, and mostly distorts the true story.

To narrate the history of a people who have mainly kept to themsleves behind the scenes, and who in addition have gone to extraordinary lengths to erase their personal and collective history from the memory of their fellow men, is no mean task. Matters are further complicated by the fact that Toltecs are seers

* *Common Era.*

who base their knowledge upon what they *see**, and since this does not often coincide with the theories of orthodox science, their rendition of Toltec history seems to become ever more irrational as it is traced back in time.

In order to grasp not only the origins of Toltecs, but also the true nature of their teachings, the utmost care must be taken not to try to place Toltecs within any frame of reference other than their own. Contrary to what mankind presently believes, there are frames of reference different to the one commonly adhered to by most of the western world. Toltecs, as well as their origin and purpose, must be seen in their own context if their teachings are to have any meaning at all. This is not to infer that Toltecs are dogmatically adhering only to their own particular doctrines, but rather that Toltecs recognize and move within many frames of reference across the barriers of time. Fantastic as it may sound, Toltecs utilize four dimensions, and thus cannot be understood within a frame of reference which is strictly three-dimensional.

The decision to disclose to the world at large the true story of the Toltecs was not a decision accompanied by the naive belief that the world would simply embrace their story as undeniable fact. Toltecs are clearly aware that humanity, being as yet three-dimensional and as such bound by the concepts of time and space, will instinctively view the Toltec story with scepticism. However, Toltecs are who and what they are simply because they have never been of a kind to be affected by public opinion. The motto of Toltecs is that *truth is more important than public belief, and any man who feels the need to adjust his knowledge so as to receive public approval is a man unworthy of trust.* It is then in the spirit of this motto, and without any attempt at justification, that this account of Toltec history and knowledge is freely offered, allowing the reader to decide for him or herself whether or not to believe what is stated.

---

* *The ability to access knowledge by arcane means.*
This concept will be explained more fully in later volumes.

This book is firstly for the thinkers of the world who have seen for themselves that humanity cannot continue indefinitely upon its present course, and that a drastic change in human attitudes and thinking is necessary if world prosperity is to be ensured. Secondly, it is for those to whom the truth is more important than words, who believe that experiential knowledge is life's priceless gift, and who acknowledge the interrelationship, interdependence and interaction of all life. But perhaps most important of all, this book is for those who have up until now been seeking a truth they sense exists, but which they have not yet been able to find. These are the truly gentle souls who do not despair, but who wait patiently in true humility. Maintaining within their hearts the quietness of life, these people know that their opportunity will one day come.

Since the task of having to write this book has fallen upon me at a time when it would seem that credentials matter more than the man himself, I could not help but wonder what sort of qualifications would be deemed acceptable for this purpose. Realising that neither my academic qualifications nor my career seem to have any overt connection with the tale it is my duty to tell, I decided to turn my attention to the current vogue in this kind of literature. What I found baffled me enormously, for it soon became clear that current credibility appears to be focused upon books channeled by either discarnate beings or extra-terrestrial intelligences.

In view of this amazing discovery, let me hasten to state that I am neither discarnate nor extra-terrestrial, but a living man of flesh and blood just like any other man walking this earth. Furthermore, I do not see myself as being particularly gifted or extraordinary in any way whatsoever, except that I am a product of the Toltec Tradition. Nevertheless it never ceases to amaze me that even though this tradition is a system of teaching as old as humanity itself, yet stories concerning it still seem to fill most people with a sense of awe and fear. The reason for this is that although the Toltec teachings are the natural heritage of mankind, humanity in general has until now not been ready to receive them. Consequently, my people have acted as custodians of this tradition since time immemorial, and have thereby, fortunately or unfortunately, earned for themselves the dubious honorific of 'sorcerers'.

It would then appear that the uncertain title of 'sorcerer' is also the qualification I have inherited by virtue of my descendancy. But as sorcery normally raises eyebrows in polite circles, and as sorcerers are generally regarded as being just a little suspect, it would perhaps have been somewhat more expedient to have claimed discarnate or extra-terrestrial status, as this could possibly have engendered more credibility and respect.

Such an option could have seemed tempting, if it were not for the fact that I fail to understand why discarnate or extra-terrestrial beings should in some miraculous way be more trustworthy than plain common-thinking human mortals. After all, if a man is a liar whilst in a physical body, why should he suddenly speak the gospel truth once he is disembodied? Likewise, who in their right minds would trust an extra-terrestrial being, who is totally unknown, to be unequivocally superior to mankind in intelligence? Such logic makes little sense, and since this book is being offered to sane sensible people, it would perhaps be more profitable not to confuse an already obscure issue with even more ambiguity.

Since in the final analysis I have then been unable to come up with anything concrete which can possibly substantiate my authority to write this book, I will present just my plain human self. Nevertheless, I shall endeavour not to become boring in my ordinariness.

Here then, without any further ado, is the story of my people.

PART ONE

THE BEGINNING OF TIME

WOLF

'.... and they shall be known as the Wolf People. In their hearts they shall carry always the vague memory of a bygone world, an orange-red sun which was once to man home, which was once both his glory and his honour. By day they shall flee the abominations of hu-man madness, and at night they shall look upon the faint light of the moon and cry out their anguish over a freedom lost, a spear and a sword forgotten. Within every fibre of their being they shall nurture for ever the ecstasy of hope and of freedom'.

Extract from the prophecies of The Nameless One.

(Black & white watercolour: Susan Emily)

CHAPTER ONE

ORIGIN OF THE TOLTEC WARRIORS AND THEIR KNOWLEDGE

'There are, scattered throughout the world, a handful of thoughtful and solitary students, who pass their lives in obscurity, far from the rumours of the world, studying the great problems of the physical and spiritual universes. They have their secret records in which are preserved the fruits of the scholastic labours of the long line of recluses whose successors they are.'

H.P. BLAVATSKY[1]

For those amongst us who prefer things to be done in the accepted manner, let me begin this account in the age-old fashion which I am sure will more than likely be deemed proper for a tale such as this.

Once upon a time..............eighteen million years ago, several groups of people, who would by today's standards be known as priests and priestesses of the ancient temples of humanity, came to this world together with mankind as we know mankind today. How this all came about and from where mankind originated are questions that go far beyond the scope of this book, but what can be said is that the arrival of man upon this planet was something akin to a semi-voluntary exile from his home-world. This planet, however, imposed such severe limitations upon the life-forms which came here that man became utterly immersed in that prison we have come to call matter. So drastic was the effect of this that man even forgot his home-world and who and what he really is. Lost and bewildered, mankind turned to the priests and priestesses for spiritual guidance, only to find that they too had been affected in the same adverse way as the rest of mankind. This was a dark period of seemingly endless struggle and hopelessness.

All of this took place in that far distant time when humanity was at that stage of evolution which is today known as Lemurian and was living upon the ancient continent of Shalmali. The immersion in matter, and man's struggle against the debilitating effect of this, took place over millions of years. In this time there were seven sub-races born within the civilization of Lemuria. The fourth sub-race of the Lemurians was known as the Barhishads, or Divine Hermaphrodites, and it was from these that there was born the Rmoahal Race, the first sub-race of the Atlanteans. From the Rmoahals were born the Tlavatli, and it was from within this stock that the priests and priestesses of old began to incarnate and slowly to regain some of their former memories.

As they gradually regained their memories, so the priests and priestesses once again began to lead their people, and so it was that they became known as Toltecs, meaning men and women of knowledge. As more of their memories were restored, the Toltecs then took it upon themselves to lead mankind back to its true home as soon as this was possible. Thus it was that they also became known as warriors of the Spirit fighting for freedom.

So this was how the history of the Toltec warriors began upon this planet in an era when mankind was just beginning to measure time as we know time today. On recalling their former training, the Toltecs began developing the ability to *see*, for they were equipped with what is today known as the third eye. It was only in the period of becoming immersed in matter and the resultant loss of memory that the Toltec seers experienced a temporary psychic blindness. However, once some of them began to remember, this natural ability to *see* returned and enabled them rapidly to recall the former knowledge they had acquired upon their home-world.

This knowledge consisted almost entirely of what is called *will-power*, mathematics, astronomy and astrology. So adept were the Toltecs in the use of *will-power* that they had no difficulty in levitating either themselves or solid objects of immense size and weight, and it was this ability which was much later used to build structures such as the Great Pyramids in Egypt and Stonehenge in England.

The Toltecs then started to teach their fellow men the mundane but practical crafts required for physical prosperity, such as fishing, hunting, cooking, healing, building, the fundamentals of mathematics, and many of the arts, notably sculpture. The Toltecs had one serious problem though, for although their knowledge was extremely comprehensive, it was as yet entirely atavistic and of another world.

The Toltecs had little understanding of the intricacies of life upon the physical plane, for even though they had already spent millions of years upon the earth, this time meant practically nothing to them because of their initial loss of memory. As a consequence, their knowledge of matter was limited. Toltecs at this time had no understanding of the abstract, for they *saw* things entirely as they were, and therefore for them everything was very clear, but nevertheless also one-sided. Due to this limitation Toltecs did not grasp the implications of duality, or its purpose. As a result, concepts such as the interrelationship and the interaction of all life, although instinctively practised by them, were not understood. In time this ignorance of the abstract was to lead to the first downfall of the Toltecs, for it gave rise to the worst form of selfishness imaginable.

For thousands of years the Toltecs led their people superbly, and the whole of their world, by then known as Atlantis, prospered in great material wealth and power. It was from this rule by the Toltecs that their world derived its name, for the word *atl* means 'head' or 'ruler'.

The people of Atlantis had an Emperor, known as the White Emperor by virtue of the fact that his knowledge was the greatest amongst the Toltecs, and as such he was likened to a great white light. The Emperor ruled his people from the capital city of the Toltecs, known as the City of the Golden Gates.

Because the crafts they had been taught by the Toltecs were specialized, the people had been divided into clans, much like guilds, and each of these guilds was governed by a small group of Toltecs. These clans lived in cities, each city being governed by a senior Toltec who had a status equivalent to a king. These kings in turn were ruled by the Emperor, who was surrounded by a group of the more learned and powerful of the Toltecs.

As time went on, and as the knowledge of the people grew, so some of the clans, together with their kings, became ambitious for more knowledge and power. No longer content with the knowledge and the power they had, these people started to look at their neighbours and more advanced Toltecs with envy. It was not long before greed drove some of the Toltecs to start experimenting with ways in which to increase their psychic abilities in an attempt to gain superiority over others. This was the beginning of sorcery, and the practice of the black art.

Having no real grasp of the abstract, Toltecs on the whole did not understand their psychic abilities any more than a duck understands how it swims. Consequently, the Toltecs who turned their hand to sorcery began to develop the most elaborate and intricate rituals with which to boost their *power**.

Even though they did not realise that these rituals served no purpose other than to strengthen their *will**, these sorcerers nevertheless managed to increase their *power* to such an extent that they began to overrun and dominate other cities and Toltecs. Rebellion and strife spread rapidly as Toltec fought

---

* *Will and power are synonymous terms for the product of perception. See Chapter 4.*

Toltec for supremacy. Warfare had been discovered and launched full-scale, but as this was a war fought not only with physical weapons but also with psychic weapons, the destruction was terrible.

The White Emperor and his group of Toltec advisors were eventually driven from the City of the Golden Gates, after which the sorcerers put one of their own upon the throne.

The White Emperor, his advisors, and many of the kings, were by this time sufficiently aware of the interrelationship of all life, and could therefore foresee the consequences of sorcery. This led to the start of the great Toltec migration, for the White Emperor and his followers started to move north into Egypt, and west into North and South America in an attempt to save themselves and their people from the disasters they could foresee.

So great had become the black Toltecs' command over the forces of nature, and so limited was their understanding of the interrelationship of all, that it did not take them long to unbalance the forces of the earth to such an extent that natural cataclysms started to occur.

The first great catastrophe struck in approximately 800,000 B.C.E. The cataclysm of earthquakes and tidal waves shattered the main continent into a great many islands of varying size and destroyed the City of the Golden Gates, together with the Black Emperor and his sorcerers. For a while this warning kept sorcery at bay, but relatively speaking it was not too long before greed once again surfaced, and in approximately 200,000 B.C.E. the second great cataclysm reduced the remains of Atlantis down to two huge islands, Daitya and Ruta.

This time the warning was not heeded for quite so long. The Toltecs upon Ruta, by then hopelessly addicted to the black art, brought about another cataclysm in 75,000 B.C.E., destroying both Ruta and Daitya, and heaving up the large island that was to become known as Poseidonis. In 9,564 B.C.E., Poseidonis also met its fate as it sank beneath massive tidal waves brought about by violent volcanic eruptions. Atlantis and her black sorcerers were finally gone forever.

At various times during the destruction of the mother continent the remnants of the Atlanteans migrated to other parts of the world, some of which had emerged as a result of the major cataclysms that destroyed Atlantis.

On the whole, these remnants, led and guided by their Toltec kings and priests, did not fare at all well. Some, however, did manage to find lands where they could settle and even flourish. Notable amongst those who prospered were the Egyptian dynasties, the Chaldeans, Peruvians, Akkadians, Tibetans, and to a lesser extent various smaller groups scattered throughout Europe, Asia and Africa.

It is not the purpose of this book to give detailed accounts of all these various lines, but merely to point out how it came about that Toltecs became so scattered throughout the world. Even to this day Toltecs are found the world over, and it is due to this fact that at least some of the lines managed to survive the rigours of the subsequent centuries.

In time, most of the weaker lines lost their Toltec kings and priests, either through wars or natural causes. Where there were no descendants of the seers the people started to fall into barbaric ignorance. This same fate also befell many of the stronger lines, and in time they too were likewise impoverished.

The number of truly learned seers diminished rapidly as finding and training suitable successors became increasingly difficult. The atavistic abilities of the original seers had moreover started to die out due to the steady development of the rational mind. This development of rational thought had become necessary in order to gain greater knowledge of the abstract, of matter and of the forces of duality.

By the time Poseidonis met its end there were only a handful of natural seers left in the world, and in time these too died out. This meant that most of the Toltec descendants, although extremely knowledgeable and capable of leading, were now no longer seers.

This lack of seers was obviously a serious setback. In their endeavour to regain the abilities of their ancestors, the Toltecs used their knowledge of medicinal plants and drugs to enable them to *see*. The drugs worked after a fashion, but the cost to the physical body and brain from using these plants continuously was soon found to outweigh the benefits. Even so, Toltecs had no other means by which to *see*, and although the rate of mortality, insanity and failure kept escalating, they desperately continued with their experiments.

Dark and terrible as this time was, it nevertheless brought Toltecs face to face with the hard facts of life on the physical plane, and thus the effects brought about by the necessary development of the rational mind finally caught up with the Toltecs, exacting a heavy toll. Yet this also meant that even though Toltecs had lost their atavistic abilities, they were for the first time faced with the opportunity to discover what those abilities had really consisted of in the first place, and exactly how these worked in practice.

It was not until much later that Toltecs could see in retrospect what a gift this dark time had been, for it was during this period of constant struggle and failure that they learned to look deep within themselves and to find there faculties they never knew they possessed. Without realising it at the time, Toltecs had taken a huge step forward in their development and had in addition defined one of the fundamentals of the Toltec Path, namely that *a warrior lives by challenge*.

As time went on, Toltecs became more selective in their use of drugs, and therefore more proficient. The rate of failure and mortality started to decline, whilst the numbers of seers increased. But by this time Toltecs were faced with yet another problem; one which was so subtle that they did not identify what it was until it was already too late.

Toltecs had become obsessed with their desire to *see* to such an extent that seeing had become for them more important than knowledge itself. With this obsession, the sobriety of their former knowledge quickly became replaced by the same arrogance and self-importance that had been the downfall of the sorcerers in Atlantis. The black art had once again reared its ugly head, and now even the remaining Toltecs succumbed to sorcery. This was the era which Carlos Castaneda describes in his books as that of the Old Seers.

Using their newly rediscovered ability to *see*, the Old Seers began reviving most of the old practices, and it did not take them long to reinstate the rituals and incantations which had been the specialized knowledge of the sorcerers of Atlantis.

These rituals allowed the Old Seers to manipulate their awareness in such a manner that they could achieve what we today call *altered states of perception*. By using these rituals and entering into different states of awareness, the Old Seers learned an enormous amount, not only about themselves but also about the other life-forms, both *organic** and *inorganic*†, which share the planet with man. Like their Atlantean predecessors, the Old Seers were remarkably clever at amassing facts and information but, since their sense of self-importance was so great, the Old Seers used this knowledge to dominate and manipulate everyone and everything luckless enough to catch their attention.

During this period in Toltec history the Old Seers re-established themselves to a great extent within the same clan or guild systems that had been in use in ancient Atlantis. So powerful were these guilds that they invariably dominated even the leaders of the people, whether king or emperor. This was equally true regardless of where in the world Toltec history was unfolding.

In this respect it should be realised that the Toltec civilization in the Valley of Mexico as described by Carlos

---

* *Life-forms which have biological functions.*

† *Life-forms which do not have biological functions.*

Castaneda was but one of many later civilizations. Historically this was the only lineage that went under the name of Toltec but, as has been explained previously, all civilizations the world over, whatever their name, had their roots in Toltec migrations from Atlantis. Therefore, at the core of all these civilizations were priest-seers trained in the Toltec tradition. As a result of this common heritage and tradition, and in spite of the fact that dates obviously vary enormously between one civilization and the next, Toltec knowledge the world over has nevertheless always unfolded in more or less an identical pattern.

The Old Seers ruled for a long period during which they continued to gather a vast amount of information about the manipulation of awareness, but they mostly used this knowledge for the furtherance of the black art. Many of the rituals and magical incantations found in the world today are watered-down versions of the techniques that were used at one time or another by these Old Seers.

Sorcery flourished and, depending upon which civilization they happened to be a part of, many of these Old Seers lasted right up until, and even beyond, the advent of Christ and the Christian Church. It was because of the unscrupulous actions and the unwholesome pursuits of these Old Seers that the Christian Church began its great persecution of paganism.

It was, however, not only the Christian Church, as is commonly assumed, that brought about the demise of the Old Seers. Even in the absence of the Christians, the Old Seers often found themselves at the mercy of other conquerors. The reason for this was that although the Old Seers had become just as powerful as their Atlantean predecessors, they still had one serious disadvantage which they had not managed to overcome.

This disadvantage amounted to the fact that the Old Seers could not entirely master the force of *will*, which the old Atlanteans had done with such ease. This was in many ways a blessing, for if the Old Seers had conquered the force of *will*, the evils of Atlantis would have been repeated, since the Old Seers would undoubtedly have unleashed upon their enemies the full force of their knowledge.

It was this lack of being able to command *will* which saved the world from yet more psychic warfare and which ultimately brought about the destruction of the Old Seers. Powerful as the Old Seers' rituals were, they were also cumbersome and impractical. Whenever physically confronted by their enemies, the lack of the necessary time in which to incant and perform their rituals rendered the Old Seers just as defenceless as the people they ruled.

During these times of trouble, and especially during the persecution of paganism by the Christian Church, some of the more far-sighted Toltecs broke away from their age-old tradition and began to review their situation within the world. These were the Toltecs which marked the beginning of that era Carlos Castaneda termed the age of the New Seers.

The New Seers could clearly see the disadvantages of lengthy and cumbersome rituals. But more important still was the fact that they could also see the futility of trying to control and manipulate others, because of the continuous strife which this inevitably brings about. This split in the Toltec tradition was by far the most important event in the history of the Toltecs, for it constituted that turning point in their knowledge, and provided that magical key which Toltecs had been seeking ever since the destruction of Atlantis.

As has already been stated, the Old Seers had enough knowledge and ability to manipulate the awareness of their victims, and this they did without scruple. The fact that awareness can be manipulated is a vitally important tenet of Toltec knowledge, but man is today generally still sceptical about this truth. Although arts such as telepathy and hypnosis have done much to eradicate this scepticism, man still finds it hard to believe that someone can manipulate his awareness without his consent or knowledge. Yet this is exactly what the Old Seers had been capable of doing.

Today Toltecs no longer adhere to the endless techniques of the Old Seers, for although these techniques remain powerful tools, they have nevertheless outlived their purpose. However, in spite of the fact that Toltecs now spurn this aspect of their heritage, these techniques still form an integral part of their knowledge, by virtue of tradition.

Another important fact to be stressed is that Toltec knowledge, because of a peculiarity of the Toltec tradition, has never been and can never be lost. This has always been one of the strengths of the Toltecs, since this accumulated knowledge has been the principal medium through which they have been able to acquire their *power*. However, for the Old Seers, as we have seen, it was also their weakness, for it was this part of the Toltec tradition which tempted them back into the abominations of the Atlantean sorcerers. In their arrogance and conceit the Old Seers aspired to a kind of *power* which was abusive, and although it would in some respects be an exaggeration to label the Old Seers as evil, they came close enough to being exactly that.

One of the most costly mistakes the Old Seers made was to fail to acknowledge the importance of having to make their knowledge more streamlined and practical for use upon the physical plane. Instead, owing to their self-importance and obsession with power, their methods of manipulating awareness became ever more complex and impractical. Furthermore, the Old Seers were far too lazy to bring any order into their already vast and rapidly-growing knowledge. Eventually it came to the point where they could no longer see the wood for the trees. Self-importance had undermined their strength, so that even though they had at their disposal knowledge that was quite awesome, chaos precluded them from being able to put it to any real practical use.

Although today we no longer condone the aberrations of the Old Seers, we must give the devil his due, for the Old Seers discovered some truly amazing facts about awareness – knowledge without which the Toltec tradition would be much impoverished.

The task that faced the New Seers was to take stock of their overburdened tradition and to re-evaluate their vast heritage of knowledge. From their experience the New Seers could see that the Old Seers had gone very far astray, but, so vast was their knowledge by this time and so utterly chaotic, that none of the New Seers were sure what was valid and what was useless. The only logical thing they could do was to start working from the hypothesis that everything their predecessors had done was questionable, and to start classifying the immense amount of knowledge available to them. This marked the end of chaos and the beginning of a long-needed order and sense of sobriety.

The New Seers discarded all the many theories the Old Seers had formulated and held as being central to their knowledge, and began searching for practical ways in which to apply this knowledge. Consequently they managed to condense the greater part of their heritage into a few fundamental concepts which could be applied practically.

The first of these concepts concerned what the Old Seers called the *Eagle*. In their attempts to fathom the purpose of existence, the Old Seers actually managed to *see* the source of all life, which when interpreted by the rational mind resembles something akin to a black and white eagle. Consequently, the Old Seers metaphorically termed this source the Eagle.

Seeing the Eagle was an act which cost a great many of the

Old Seers their sanity, or their lives, or both. However, from what they managed to *see* they worked out that the purpose of existence is to enhance the quality of awareness. This was an invaluable discovery, and one which has become fundamental to everything that Toltecs today know and practise.

The Old Seers could *see* that it is the Eagle which endows all beings with awareness at the moment of birth and which also reclaims this awareness at the moment of death, having become enriched by the being's experiences during life. The Old Seers understood this as meaning that the Eagle feeds off awareness, and that the sole purpose of existence is therefore to keep recycling awareness so as to bring out all latent potential.

It is important to realise that there is of course no Eagle as such, nor is there anything visual about the incomprehensible source of life. Nevertheless, even a seer is subjected to the conditions of the rational mind, which must by its very nature interpret things, and the result of such interpretation is a visual impact of the Eagle.

The manifested universe is an infinity beyond our understanding of time and space, for its size and complexity cannot be rendered comprehensible in terms of words or mortal concepts. It is not God, for God after all is part of what we know. The churches, ministers of religion, and even other people, are constantly trying to describe God to us, so therefore God becomes something within the scope of words, within the sphere of conceptualization. But beyond words, beyond description, beyond concept, lies that indescribable, incomprehensible No-Thing, which can only be termed the Unspeakable.

This was yet another error on the part of the Old Seers. In their arrogance they never stopped to consider that most of what constitutes the manifested universe is utterly incomprehensible and unknowable within the framework of our human condition. The New Seers corrected this mistake by identifying and demarcating three distinct levels of awareness.

The first of these levels they termed the *known*, which

consists of everything the human being can register within normal awareness. The second level, termed the *unknown*, is a truly vast and mysterious area, but which can and does become the known gradually and sequentially as the seer gains in his proficiency to see it. The third level, on the other hand, termed the *unknowable*, is a level of awareness which can never be known to man whilst he still retains his humanness. To enter into the unknowable is to lose our humanness, which is why so many of the Old Seers lost their sanity.

The Old Seers had, over generations, gathered a vast number of facts about awareness, which they never formulated into an ordered structure. As the New Seers started to rearrange these facts another very important set of concepts emerged, which were condensed into an ordered whole to form a set of precepts which were termed the *Truths of Awareness.* The New Seers regarded these precepts as paramount to all of their understanding, and to this day these *truths* form the foundations of the Toltec Teachings.

Most of the Truths of Awareness are based upon the *act of perception* and the way in which this takes place. The New Seers found that the whole mystery of perception can be summarized quite adequately in the following nine precepts:

1. The universe consists of an infinite number of energy fields resembling threads of light.

2. These threadlike energy fields radiate from a source of unimaginable dimensions metaphorically called the Eagle. As such these energy fields are known as the Eagle's Emanations.

3. Human beings are likewise composed of the same infinite number of these threadlike energy fields which manifest in the shape of a large luminous egg. The height of this egg is equal to the length of a man's body with his arms fully extended above his head on the vertical axis, and its width is that of a man with his arms extended outwards from the centre of his body along the horizontal axis. This egg is known as the cocoon of man.

4. Only a small group of the energy fields inside the cocoon are lit up at any one time by a brilliant point of light located on the surface of the cocoon.

5. Perception takes place when the energy fields which are illuminated by the point of light extend their light to illuminate corresponding energy fields outside the cocoon. This point of light is termed the point where perception is assembled, normally abbreviated to the assemblage point.

6. It is possible to shift the assemblage point to any other position on the surface of the cocoon, or even into its interior. Because the assemblage point illuminates any energy fields with which it comes into contact, the new energy fields it illuminates as a result of such shifting constitute therefore a new perception. It is this new level of perception that is known as ***seeing****.*

7. When the assemblage point shifts sufficiently far a totally new world is perceived, which is as real as the one man normally perceives.

8. There is a mysterious force known as ***intent*** *which exists throughout the entire universe. It is this force which brings about perception, for it is* ***intent*** *which, firstly, aligns the energy fields, and secondly, causes awareness of that alignment.*

9. The goal of warriors is to experience all possible perceptions available to man. This constitutes what is known as **Total Awareness**, *inherent within which is an alternate way of dying.*

In order to *see*, the Old Seers had to use hallucinogens to move their assemblage points, but the New Seers realised that this was as impractical as the rituals of the Old Seers. More than anything else, practical ways of moving the assemblage point were now needed, and in order to find these the New Seers began by studying the assemblage point through *seeing*, even though at the outset they still had to make use of drugs. This research turned out to be most worthwhile, for not only did they find the necessary techniques to enable them to move the assemblage point, but they also uncovered the mystery of will-power.

The Old Seers had known about the mysterious force which their Atlantean predecessors had used with such facility. Through observation, they also knew that this force exists throughout all of nature and the manifested universe. The Old Seers termed this force *power*, but they never understood it or managed to figure out how to use it.

The New Seers discovered that this mysterious force is in fact the *energy of alignment*, that is, the force that is released when energy fields inside the cocoon become aligned with energy fields outside the cocoon. The New Seers termed this force *will*, and defined it as 'a continuous flow of energy which can be guided by the *intent* of the seer'.

The New Seers also discovered that *will* is the force that makes us behave in the ways we do when we perceive. It is therefore this force that determines our perception of the world. Thus it is *will* which fixes the assemblage point at the exact spot where it is located. Here it is important to realise that although there is a definite area within which the assemblage point can always be found, the exact position is brought about by habitual action and repetition. Habits obviously vary between one individual and the next, and consequently no two people will have their assemblage points fixed in exactly the same spot.

The assemblage point of man is generally found on the surface of the cocoon, roughly opposite the point between the shoulder blades. In the development of the normal child, the child first learns where it seems most suitable to place the assemblage point and then fixes it there through repetition. This repetition is at first mostly dictated by encouragement from elders and later by habitual internal dialogue. Toltecs today know that man can only maintain his view of the world by constantly confirming this view to himself by means of his internal dialogue. This means that the world always appears to be exactly what man constantly tells himself it is.

By far the most important aspect of Toltec knowledge is that once the internal dialogue has been stopped the assemblage point is free to move. This enables man to experience altered states of perception quite spontaneously and is the magical key the Old Seers had searched for so ardently. Had they but realised that the only real value of their rituals lay in their ability to shift the assemblage point the Old Seers would have discovered this key, as well as the secret of *will* or *power*.

Once this discovery had been made, Toltec knowledge became transformed, and the New Seers were well on their way to correcting the mistakes of their predecessors.

In order to move the assemblage point, the New Seers defined three principal techniques based upon the nine Truths of Awareness. The first technique is termed the *Art of Stalking*, the second is the *Art of Dreaming* and the third is the *Mastery of Intent*. From these three techniques evolved three distinct areas of activity in which every apprentice must become totally proficient if he is to succeed in becoming a Toltec – namely, the *Art of Stalking*, the *Mastery of Awareness* and the *Mastery of Intent*. In this scheme the Art of Dreaming is incorporated into the Mastery of Awareness and is used only as a means by which the assemblage point can be moved in order to achieve altered states of perception.

These three areas of activity have been defined traditionally as the three riddles which warriors must face and answer as they walk the Path of Power. The Art of Stalking is termed the *riddle of the heart*. It is described as the bafflement warriors experience when they become aware, firstly, that the world appears to be what it is only because of our perception and, secondly, that if a different perception is brought to bear upon the world, then our view of the world, which seems to be so inviolable, changes dramatically. The Mastery of Awareness is termed the *riddle of the mind*. This is the awesome infinity warriors perceive when they realise the incomprehensible mystery and extent of man's awareness. The Mastery of Intent is the *riddle of the spirit of man*. It is the ultimate paradox in that it is the ability of man to project his actions, physical, emotional and mental, beyond normal human comprehension.

As far as the process of learning is concerned, the most important discovery of the New Seers was something which the Old Seers had already uncovered, namely that man has two types of awareness, which they termed the *right* and *left* side of man. The right side is the thinking, logical, rational side of man's mind. On the right side all knowledge flows in a linear and sequential mode. The left side, on the other hand, is the feeling, irrational side of man's mind which operates entirely independently of any logical or linear progression of sequential thought patterns. The best way in which to understand the right side, as opposed to the left side, is to consider an example of each.

Consider a mother who receives a telephone call informing her that her son has had an accident. On the right side the mother will experience more or less the following:

The telephone rings and the mother answers it not expecting anything untoward. When told of the accident she first experiences shock and fear, then concern for her son's safety. Many questions flood through her mind in sequence; 'Is he hurt? Where is he? What happened? Is he in hospital?'

This is a very simplified, but nonetheless typically logical reaction in which one thought triggers off another. But had the mother been able to register the left side, her experience would have been completely different and something like the following:

Before her son left home that morning the mother had an uneasy feeling concerning his safety, and even though there was no logical reason why she should feel uncomfortable, she could not shake off the feeling. Then suddenly, mid-morning, she experiences a feeling of alarm. In that moment she senses the presence of her son and can feel that he is deeply distressed. The mother does not pause to question this, but instinctively starts walking towards the telephone, wondering how best she may reach her son or someone who can put her mind at rest. Even before she reaches the telephone it rings, and as she picks up the receiver a cold shiver runs down her spine, for she knows she is going to hear that her son has had an accident. However, even as she answers the telephone, the mother somehow knows that he is not seriously injured, just shocked.

From these two examples it is plain to see the difference between right and left. The right is a rational reaction to concrete evidence which sets up a sequence of logical thoughts; the left is an irrational feeling which has nothing to do with either logic or concrete evidence to begin with. Only later will such irrational feelings be corroborated by the necessary evidence. In trying to understand these concepts it is important to realise that the terms 'right' and 'left side' are terms used for the luminous cocoon of man, and not the right and left hemispheres of the brain and their respective functions.

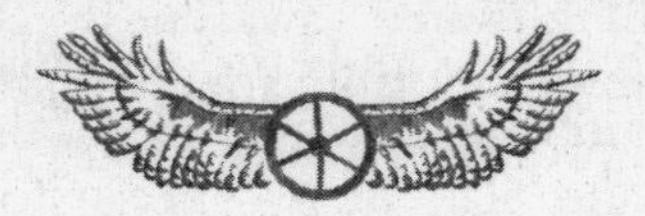

The Old Seers termed the left side *heightened awareness*, and since the absence of logical thought enhances clarity, they used to force their apprentices into this state so that the apprentices could achieve the level of concentration required in order to learn sorcery. The only justification for this method of teaching lies in the fact that the apprentice has great difficulty in remembering teachings communicated to him whilst in a state of heightened awareness. This lack of memory creates a kind of obstacle course, since before the apprentice can utilize his knowledge he has to struggle to recall it. Such a struggle often takes years and, as a result, by the time the apprentice does remember the teachings, he has, through his long struggle, become totally committed to them.

Today Toltecs have a different view, for now we know that man always learns upon both levels simultaneously. However, learning and remembering what we have learned requires energy, just like anything else. This creates a problem in that the vast majority of people simply do not have enough energy to register what they are learning on the left side as well as on the right side.

Sometimes a person's energy is at such a low ebb that he cannot even remember what he has learned on the right side, let alone also the left side. Because of a peculiarity of our awareness, the right side always takes precedence over the left side. All available energy is primarily used firstly to register, and secondly to recollect the right side. Only surplus energy is used for the left side.

In the teaching scheme in use today, apprentices are very rarely forced into heightened awareness simply because the time factor involved in recollecting is too costly. From the very first day of their training apprentices are given instruction which enables them to bring about a natural and spontaneous movement into heightened awareness. Although in the beginning such a movement is invariably minute, the apprentice soon begins to gain proficiency in this art. Consequently, as the apprentice gains in the ability to move deeper into heightened awareness, so the instruction given is stepped up in complexity.

This new method has two great advantages: firstly, the apprentice learns right from the beginning to handle his own awareness, and secondly, time is not lost in lengthy recollections.

This very briefly outlines the new approach and teaching scheme the New Seers constructed out of the knowledge they inherited from their tradition. The New Seers' work was just beginning to take effect when the Christian Church began its long-standing persecution of paganism.

Unhappy as this persecution was, it nonetheless provided the New Seers with the unparalleled opportunity of being able to hone their new-found skills into instruments of the most exacting precision. Mistakes and sloppy technique resulted in torture and death at the hands of the persecutors. Those warriors who were slow to learn, or were just not proficient enough in their new skills, died very quickly. This was a most uncompromising period in the history of the Toltecs, for although they were forced into learning excellence, the persecution in most parts of the world was so devastating that Toltecs everywhere had to make some far-reaching decisions.

In their attempts to survive, Toltecs the world over at one time or another during the following centuries took the decision to disband. Consequently, every leader dissociated himself and his unit from all other units. This was a drastic move which not only resulted in the founding of the different lineages, but which also brought about, for the first time in Toltec history, the isolated development of knowledge.

This move and its effects have become known as the Doctrine of Separate Development. So far-reaching has been the ripple effect of this development that today every Toltec unit exists in solitary confinement, well-hidden from the eyes of the public. Apart from a telepathic mind-link which still exists between most Toltec leaders, there is no communication between one unit and another. However, even this mind-link is of such a tenuous nature that it is not possible for the user to establish the personal identity or physical location of another.

One more aspect of Toltec knowledge needs to be understood at this point if the historical development of the Toltec tradition is to be grasped as a whole. The new method of teaching which is in force today has another very important advantage in that it allows for the proper instruction to be given to certain 'new' types now coming into incarnation. This point is mentioned here only as a matter of curiosity, for as yet it has no bearing upon the majority of appprentices.

These so-called new types are today still extremely rare. They are Toltecs who have undergone highly specialized training in a former incarnation and the *power* they wield is of a vastly different quality to that which is generally known. These Toltecs have been given the name Warriors of the Third Attention.

Much confusion will in the future be avoided if it is made clear that although it may appear as if all Toltecs are the same, this is not strictly true. Toltecs are classified into three distinct categories depending on their level of training and proficiency. These three categories of Toltec existence are termed *courts.* The first, or *outer court*, is comprised of what are called *Warriors of the First Attention*; the second, or *inner court*, are the *Warriors of the Second Attention*; and the third, or the *Sanctum Sanctorum* as it were, are the *Warriors of the Third Attention.*

These three courts must not be confused with what are known as the three stages in the development of a warrior, namely, the *hunter*, the *warrior* and the *man of knowledge.* Strictly speaking, these three stages tend to overlap the extent of the courts. Therefore, by going through the three stages, the apprentice first becomes a Toltec of the First Attention and from there graduates to the level of the Second Attention, and finally to the Third Attention.

This training is naturally not something which is normally possible in the space of one lifetime. Toltecs the world over have therefore moved progressively forward through the courts, although there have always been those rare individuals who have moved forward faster than most. These individuals invariably become leaders, even amongst Toltecs. For example, the Old Seers were predominantly Warriors of the First Attention, but had amongst them leaders of the Second Attention who defined for them the course of action to be followed. The New Seers were, correctly speaking, Warriors of the Second Attention, and they in turn had leaders who were beginning to master the Third Attention.

The three levels of proficiency, or courts, are better understood when the three stages in the training of an apprentice are viewed as a whole.

Every apprentice starts his training in normal awareness, termed the First Attention, because this teaching is within the grasp of everyone. It is, as it were, at the level of the average man in the street, and handles both the theory and practical application of all the basic concepts pertaining to the acquisition of knowledge or *personal power.*

This training covers every aspect of the Toltec tradition known as the *teachings for the right side*, and is generally grasped with relative ease, as it is directed at the rational mind. This section of the teachings is what is known as *The Way of the Hunter*. Proficiency in being able to master the instruction given in this section, together with the ability to move the assemblage point, earns for the apprentice the title of a Warrior of the First Attention.

Running parallel to this training is that section of the teachings which deals with awareness from the angle of heightened awareness or, more accurately, the Second Attention. In this section the apprentice is constantly being manipulated into shifting his assemblage point into left side awareness, and whilst in this state is made to review everything which has been learned in normal awareness.

It is in this section of the work that the apprentice is taught the concepts of *stalking, dreaming* and *intent*. This training covers that knowledge known as *The Way of the Warrior*, and generally prepares the apprentice for the more advanced work.

Proficiency in both the Way of the Hunter and the Way of the Warrior constitutes that knowledge which is recognized by the title of a Warrior of the Second Attention. If in addition to having mastered this section of the work the warrior is also able to *see* unaided, then he is regarded as a Toltec, which it will be remembered implies a seer, or man of knowledge.

From this point onwards the warrior no longer needs instruction as such, because everything stands revealed to his power of inner sight. However, the conferment of Toltec status at this point in the development of the warrior, although widely used in the past by the New Seers is, strictly speaking, not correct. According to tradition, such status is only justified when the seer also takes upon himself the responsiblity of leading his people.

Having reached this level in his development the warrior is already a master in his own right, and as such the next section of his training is not instruction in the normal sense of the word. Such instruction is rather guidance towards the unfolding of his full *power* and responsiblity as a magical being of the universe.

The knowledge covered in this section deals primarily with altered states of perception and their uses, together with alternate worlds and the denizens of those worlds as they interact with man. In this part of their training warriors are also guided into performing their true function as one of the four different types of men or women within a Toltec unit*, and are given instruction on the purpose and destiny of the unit and group† to which they belong.

Whilst the initial training of a warrior deals primarily with the development of the *individual*, this section of the training involves the concept of *group effort*. It has as its basis intelligent co-operation in the guiding of the race, and man's responsibility towards the other life-forms who share the planet with him. Proficiency in this section of knowledge is what truly constitutes *The Way of the Toltec*. It is the pinnacle of the Toltec Path and, if successfully completed, leads the warrior to that crossroad known as *The Ultimate Choice*.

The Ultimate Choice involves the warrior having to choose between the two paths which are available to Toltecs who reach this point in the unfoldment of their *power*. The one path is known as *The Path of Freedom*, whilst the other is termed *The Path of High Adventure*. The latter path is the paramount temptation for warriors, for it is a brilliant and most enticing path offering its devotees dazzling power which can only be described as intoxicating, but it does not lead warriors to freedom.

Followers of The Path of High Adventure develop the Second Attention to its ultimate potential, enabling those practioners to enlist the aid of inorganic entities, to effect

---

* *This is the technical term used for warriors working under the guidance of a nagal upon the physical plane.*

† *The awareness of mankind is divided into seven different qualities of awareness, termed groups. Units of warriors are sub-divisions of these greater groups.*

transformations of the human body, and even to slow the aging process down to such an extent as to achieve relative immortality.

On the other hand, those warriors who choose to turn away from these formidable powers continue their search, rather than becoming obsessed with the glamour of the Second Attention. In time, these warriors find themselves entering that level of awareness termed the Third Attention. These are the warriors who walk the Path of Freedom, and who are also known as *Warriors of the Third Attention*.

Warriors of the Third Attention always remain within the unit to which they belong and continue research work which cannot easily be rendered comprehensible in terms of words, for it entails the projection of thought patterns and the manipulation of awareness and perception beyond the normal comprehension of mankind. It is work which can best be described as being exclusively group orientated, but not in the sense in which this is normally understood. Suffice it to say that although all Warriors of the Third Attention have for a long, long time been working from the understanding that their power does not entitle them to interfere where they are not needed, nonetheless they have always willingly undertaken any tasks periodically assigned to them by Those they have come to call the Guardians of the Race.

As has already been mentioned, world evolution today stands at a crucial crossroad. Toltec evolution finds itself confronted by this same crisis, since the challenge facing the world is identical to the one facing the Toltecs. Today, Toltec Warriors of the Third Attention acknowledge the fact that if Toltec evolution is to proceed according to universal law, and if Toltecs are once again to take their rightful place in society, then the Doctrine of Separate Development must be spurned. Toltecs the world over must re-unite and pool their knowledge and power if Toltecs as a whole are to fulfil their true purpose in the unfolding of planetary destiny.

Likewise, if world prosperity and peace is to be established, mankind must drop its sectarianism, racialism and separativeness, and must instead adopt a universal policy which will bring all the peoples of the world and their knowledge together to form one pool of common human endeavour.

This is not to say that there must necessarily be one world government, or even for that matter one world religion, but rather that mankind must endeavour to recognize the interrelationship and interdependence of all life and of all true knowledge. There is after all but one humanity, and only one truth. What separates and divides, what causes misunderstanding and hatred, is man's inability, as yet, to recognize the fact that there is more than the one frame of reference to which he so dogmatically adheres.

If man will only pause to consider that perhaps the world is not what he has always forced himself to believe it is, then he will come to the realisation that a multiplicity of religious beliefs, or differing political ideologies, does not mean that one is right and the other is wrong, but rather that all contain one particular facet of an overall truth. Once this has been understood it is not so difficult to see that all facets are needed if the whole truth is to stand revealed. Then too will the concept of universal brotherhood not seem quite so idealistic and unachievable.

Toltecs have ever known that understanding is relative to the frame of reference used. If this frame of reference is altered, then so is our perception of the world, and for that matter, of truth. At the end of the day the only truth that is worth defending and striving for is that overall perception born from the fluidity of the assemblage point – a fluidity which is needed in order to achieve *total awareness.* This highly specialized knowledge is the gift Toltecs bring to mankind, and in their experience of handling this knowledge lies man's hope for future prosperity and world peace.

As experience has shown, such peace cannot be enforced by political treaties based upon empty promises. Lasting peace will only be achieved if it is mutually accepted by all and grounded in the universal understanding of the interrelationship and interdependence of all life.

This concept is of course far from new, for mankind has been speaking about universal brotherhood for ever and a day. However, as long as man dogmatically holds on to the idea that physical plane reality is the only frame of reference there is, he will always be fighting to make his brother accept his views, his beliefs, his ideologies, as the only ones that are correct.

The Christian Church is a prime example of this, for although there has been but one Christ bringing one message to the world, there are today so many different denominations of the Christian Church all claiming to possess the one truth that the mind boggles. In this respect, other world religions have not fared much better, especially the New Age movements and esoteric schools of thought. Anyone seeking the truth today is invariably bombarded with the most fantastic claims made by a whole host of movements and individuals who quite unscrupulously trade upon man's general confusion as to what he should be following.

In view of what has happened to mankind's religious structures, it is not so surprising that scientists the world over have more or less divorced themselves entirely from all beliefs which have their basis in ethico-religious thought. Yet here, too, Toltecs can be of invaluable assistance to science. Toltecs' knowledge of the human psyche and its reflection within the universe and in nature generally is not something which has been based upon haphazard assumption and superstition. Should orthodox science wish to do so, this knowledge can be corroborated systematically and scientifically.

The same is also true of medicine, but again it is

understandable that orthodox medicine should snort indignantly at the hocus-pocus which, unfortunately, is sometimes publicised under the name of alternative medicine. This is not to infer that alternative medicine is nonsense, but rather that there are sadly far too many ignorant people who fancy themsleves as healers.

Should mankind be willing to accept the interrelationship of all life as at least a working hypothesis, then education too will automatically undergo the much-needed and many changes necessary if it is to equip up-and-coming generations with the knowledge required in order to fulfil present and future world needs.

In all of this the world at large should today turn its attention fully to that little understood orphan of the world, namely South Africa. That strange country of mixed peoples, mixed beliefs, conflicting political ideologies and socio-economic variances has long been groping around in the darkness of human failings and despair, but in that darkness it has begun to find the hope engendered by universal reconciliation and the interdependence of all life.

In this country will be born a totally new order of human society based upon that tolerance and acceptance which comes from a people who have finally come to grasp the importance of every individual as a unit necessary to the well-being of the whole. By the year 2000 it will be to South Africa that the world will look for guidance in all matters of a humanitarian nature.

South Africa has, through its practice of gross separativeness, been brought face to face with the meaning of brotherhood and world goodwill. It is to this effect that the Guardians of the Race have bent all effort over the past few decades. Therefore, it is also in this country that Toltecs will launch their endeavour to re-unite and to resume their long-abandoned leadership in world thought.

This then concludes the account of the historical development of Toltec knowledge throughout the ages right up to the present time, and through this it is hoped that the reader now has at least some idea of the backdrop against which to view the work of Toltecs as they strive to walk the Path of Knowledge.

If one were to summarise the Toltec Path in a few words one could never do it justice, and yet perhaps one could say that ultimately it is the *Path of Power*, which is also the *Path of Freedom*. It is the Path of Power because, firstly, upon this path we learn to achieve the *power* which enables us to become aware of the hidden potentials within ourselves, and secondly, we learn to use those hidden potentials to unlock within ourselves the formidable powers of awareness and perception. Once the mystery of perception has been understood and mastered, our power and ability to bring about world peace and prosperity stands fully revealed and ready for use.

It is also the Path of Freedom, because upon this path we learn that we have a choice. We can, if we wish, remain victims of fate by doggedly holding on to our one and only view of the world. Alternatively, we can expand our awareness to include all the possible perceptions available to man and so ally ourselves with that fate. When we ally ourselves with our fate we in a sense rise above it, and thus gain a measure of freedom.

Toltecs teach that each of us has the ability and the right *to make our command the Eagle's command*, for this we say is *the Eagle's gift* to man. However, it is the rare man indeed who realises that the only thing required of us in order to accept this truly priceless gift is the knowledge and energy with which to move the assemblage point.

In this respect those of us who have dedicated our allegiance to the Guardians of the Race in helping to uplift all of life upon this planet stand ready to guide humanity however best we may. Toltecs are willing to put all their knowledge at the disposal of the world so that mankind may finally benefit from its rightful heritage. For far too long have Toltecs had to play the role of custodians of this heritage, and as such been forced to carry the heavy burden of accepting sole responsibility for their people. In the past this has been necessary, but today this is no longer true. Mankind has come of age, and thus the time is now ripe for man to accept joint responsiblity in the peaceful and successful furtherance of all evolution of life upon this magnificent planet.

Toltecs will therefore play their part in revealing to mankind what exactly its heritage entails, and so will the age-old secrets stand revealed. This book is but the first step in this direction. Now indeed is mankind's *hour of power*. This is the hour in which mankind must *seize the fleeting moment of chance* – a chance which he must not let slip if he is indeed to come into his own as the magical being of the universe which he is by divine birthright.

All of this is according to Divine Law, and thus will the ancient prophecy be fulfilled.

PART TWO

The Teachings:
FUNDAMENTAL CONCEPTS

FOX

The warrior acknowledges that there are superior forces which guide him as well as other creatures. These forces dictate the circumstances of both life and death.

(Pencil drawing: Susan Emily)

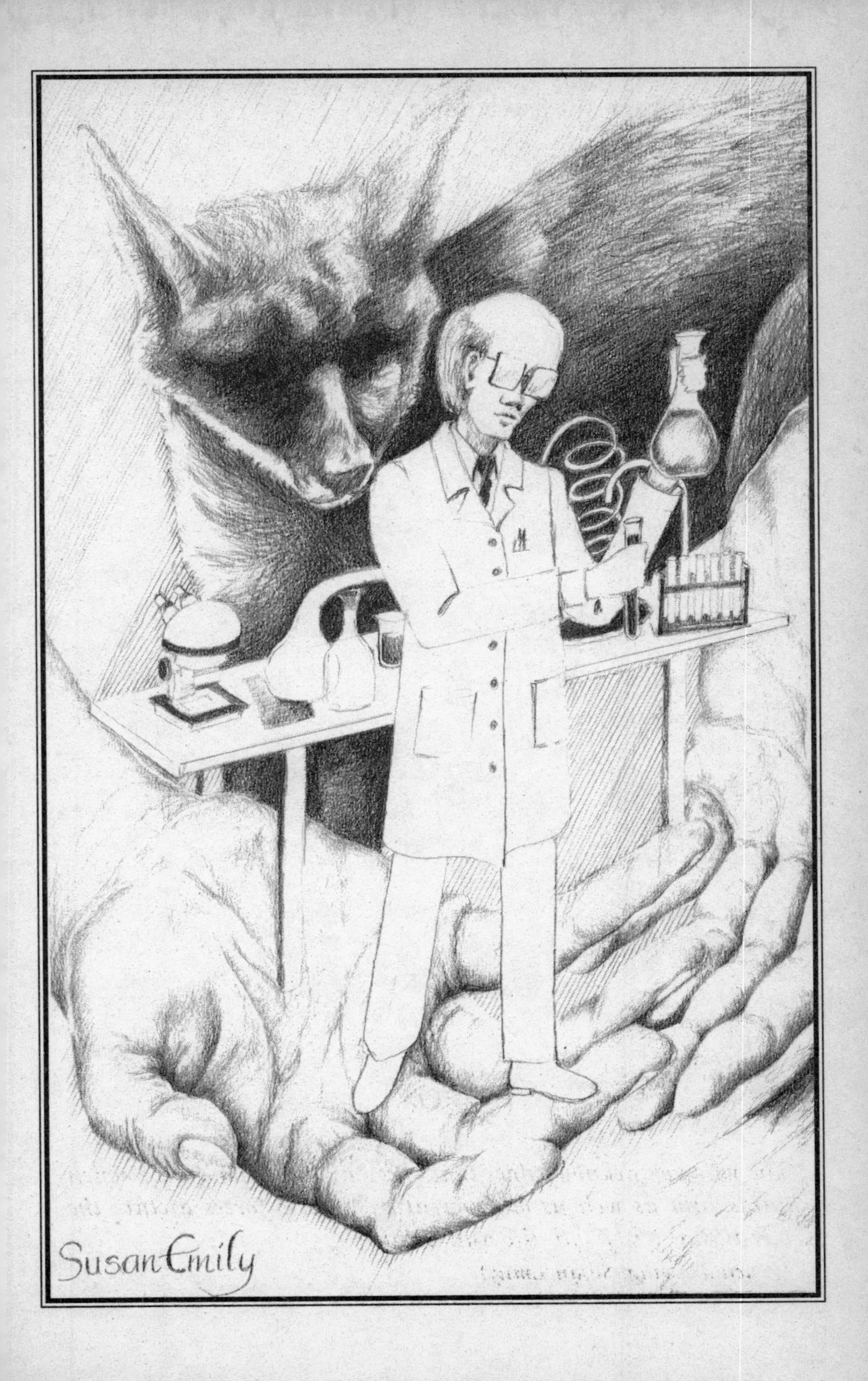
Susan Emily

CHAPTER TWO

THE PROPERTIES OF WORDS

'It takes two to tell the truth - one to tell it, the other to hear it.'

HENRY DAVID THOREAU [1]

As I have already mentioned in the introduction to this book, the Toltec teachings cannot be understood fully unless they are viewed within their own context or frame of reference. In Toltec terms such a frame of reference is called a *view of the world*, and is dependent upon the position of man's assemblage point, which under certain circumstances can be made to move, and thus bring about a different view of the world. Normally the assemblage point is firmly fixed, and so every man or woman has only one frame of reference according to which he or she naturally defines all knowledge and experience gained. For this reason it is vital that before approaching the actual teachings certain fundamental concepts are first introduced and defined.

The first concept to be covered in this way is that of words and their use. The way in which we view the world in general and knowledge in particular depends on the way in which we understand and use words. It must be stressed that words, no matter how carefully chosen, always *veil* the truth. This fact can never be over-emphasized, for again and again does man stumble over words because he does not as yet see words for the *symbols* they are, and therefore he hears and reads words in the context of his social conditioning.

THE MISTAKE OF MAN IS THAT HE ALWAYS SEEKS EXPLANATIONS WHICH UPHOLD HIS WAY OF THINKING, HIS VIEW OF THE WORLD.

When it comes to the use of words and attempting to see them for what they truly are, it must be realised that there are three kinds of bad habits man indulges in over and over again.

WHENEVER A MAN IS FACED WITH ANYTHING OUT OF THE ORDINARY HE WILL, ACCORDING TO HIS TEMPERAMENT, ALWAYS RESORT TO ONE OF THREE KINDS OF BAD HABITS:

THE BIGOT WILL IGNORE WHAT HAS HAPPENED AND PRETEND IT HAS NEVER OCCURRED.

THE SANCTIMONIOUS MAN WILL ACCEPT THE INCIDENT AT FACE VALUE, BELIEVING THAT HE UNDERSTANDS IT ALL.

THE FOOLISH MAN IS FOREVER PUZZLED BY WHAT HAS HAPPENED, NOT KNOWING WHETHER TO ACCEPT OR REJECT THE INCIDENT, AND THUS BECOMES OBSESSED WITH HIS QUESTIONS.

If the Toltec teachings are to be understood and have value for the reader, these bad habits should be studiously avoided and the stance of the warrior adopted instead.

WHEN THE WARRIOR ENCOUNTERS ANYTHING EXTRAORDINARY HE BEHAVES AS IF NOTHING HAS HAPPENED, BECAUSE HE DOES NOT BELIEVE FOR THE SAKE OF BELIEVING. ALTHOUGH THE WARRIOR ACCEPTS THE FACE VALUE OF SOMETHING, HE ALSO IGNORES IT, FOR HE KNOWS THE WORLD IS NOT WHAT IT APPEARS TO BE. THEREFORE, THE WARRIOR BEHAVES AS IF HE IS IN CONTROL, EVEN WHEN HE MAY BE TOTALLY BAFFLED, FOR BY ACTING IN THIS WAY HE AVOIDS THE CONFUSION BORN OF OBSESSION.

Let us look at how this works by taking as an example the

history of the Toltecs as explained in the first part of this book. To disregard this history as fantasy and to ignore it is to be a bigot. Alternatively, to take the narrative at its face value and to regard this as being the gospel truth is to be sanctimonious. But to become confused over which parts of the history seem to make sense and which parts appear to be unacceptable would be to become obsessed with the type of question which, when answered, only throws up more questions. Posing this type of unanswerable question is clearly an unprofitable and foolish pursuit.

The warrior, on the other hand, adopts a totally different frame of mind, for he knows full well the deceptive quality of words and the fact that they ever veil the truth. Therefore the warrior reads and listens to the words at face value but does not for one moment believe that the words in themselves are the truth he seeks. The warrior knows that words convey the truth in much the same way that a cup holds water. Obviously there is no comparison between the cup and the water it holds, just as there is no comparison between the face value of words and the truth they convey.

Let us look at the example of the term *energy field*. There is no way in which this term can possibly be taken at face value, and yet we *have* to take it at face value, for by doing so a wealth of knowledge is revealed.

The term 'energy field' conjures up for the rational mind a radiation of sorts, whether this be light, colour, sound, magnetism, electricity, awareness, or any other form of radiation. Such a field is obviously also three-dimensional, although the term itself does not give us any clue as to what form the field takes. Is it circular, oblong, threadlike, or perhaps spherical? Neither does the term tell us from where this energy originates, or what it is doing. We do not know whether it is moving linearly, pulsating, alternating, or oscillating. In short, we do not know the purpose of this energy, and therefore we do not know whether or not we should concern ourselves with it.

Furthermore, we do not know whether this energy field will be perceived differently if it is observed within the context of another frame of reference.

Clearly, the term 'energy field' is a great help in formulating our knowledge, but in itself it is totally inadequate when describing something which a seer can witness in a single moment. In truth one could write a whole thesis on that *some-thing* the seer has witnessed in its totality in one moment of perception. Then one could write another whole thesis on trying to prove what he has seen, then another on its relevance, and yet others upon its possible purpose, applications, origin, etc. After the reader of these theses has laboriously waded his way through all these endless descriptions he will still not know for sure what an energy field really is, simply because he has never seen one, nor has he experienced its effects.

If a warrior had to resort to this type of learning, he would, like the average man in the street, become hopelessly lost in a maze of meaningless words. If, on the other hand, he sees and uses words as symbols for what has been witnessed, he begins to understand that words are merely the springboard into true knowledge, or the key that grants access to a whole new world of perception.

It is for this reason that the warrior *accepts everything at face value, but does not believe in anything*. This means that the warrior disregards the *face value* of words knowing that this only veils the truth, but does *not* disregard the *words themselves*, for he knows equally well that, if they are correctly used, those words will lead him into the knowledge they veil.

Thus it is also stated that the warrior *never believes for the sake of believing, for he knows that the world is not what it appears to be*. Therefore, when hearing or reading words, the warrior knows that he is *absorbing* words which must be *fathomed* or, strictly speaking, *sounded out*.

This sounding out is what is known as *working with sound*. Working with sound is an act of the heart rather than of the mind. It entails learning to acknowledge and to trust that peculiar *feeling* which can best be described as *hearing something that rings true.*

By listening to that feeling an enormous amount of knowledge flows, knowledge which a warrior often did not know he had! But it is always at this point that the rational mind will kick in with the objection that it is all only imagination. A fine line of discrimination exists at this point – a discrimination which has rightfully been termed a double-edged sword. This discrimination can either aid the warrior in achieving clarity, or it can destroy the new knowledge gained.

Thus it is that the warrior *behaves as if he is in control, even though he may be completely baffled*, for to acknowledge this *feeling* of knowledge, and then to trust the knowledge as it arises from the heart is most threatening to the rational mind, which sees that its authority is being usurped. Consequently, the warrior experiences a fear of becoming irrational and of sinking into a quagmire of fantasy. The only way around this fear *is to act as if he is in control*, for as paradoxical as this may sound, *acting as if* is a most powerful way of placating the rational mind.

A point which needs to be emphasized here is that the so-called *imagination* is the image-forming faculty of the mind, and more, so very much more. It is a profound truth that a simple picture is worth a million words! An architect can convey everything he intends building with a few diagrams and is even more successful if he exhibits a three-dimensional model. Today these models can be done so easily by using computer graphics, but they can also be done just as well, faster, and with greater fluidity, by the image-forming faculty of the mind.

Now it is true that the model is not the finished structure upon the physical plane, and it is equally true that the mental image of knowledge is not the proven experience upon the physical plane, but in both cases it is the imagination that leads to concretization. Had Bell regarded his mental image of the telephone as being pure fantasy, he would never have been able to make a physical telephone! Likewise, if seers regarded what they *see* as the movement of the assemblage point as being fantasy, warriors today would still not be able to move their assemblage points and Toltecs, like everyone else, would be limited to only one frame of reference.

> *THE PREREQUISITE FOR A WARRIOR IS THAT HE HAS TO BELIEVE, FOR BELIEVING IS AN ESSENTIAL CONDITION OF HIS BEING.*

The fact that words are but a form of symbol for a deeper knowledge is one of the most difficult concepts to get across to anyone. In man's effort to refine his view of the world, linguists have laboured hard across a great many centuries to define and to redefine the words of language so that every word man uses today has fixed values within a prescribed context. As a result, words have acquired more importance than the knowledge they were initially intended to convey.

Today a person is judged educated or not more by the way in which he speaks than by what he is actually saying. Words have become more important than knowledge itself, and theory has won a privileged position in the life of man. In man's present view of the world it is astonishing to see the power of words and the influence of man's speech upon his world. It has been said that the universe is never ever the same again after every word spoken, and true as this is, it is even more true to say that man's view of the world becomes ever more concretized after every word spoken.

Whenever man is faced with something new or something which he cannot grasp with his rational mind he immediately sets about describing it and explaining it with words. By the time he has finished explaining it, it fits very comfortably and securely into his view of the world. Such is the power and the trap of words.

A warrior cannot avoid the use of words, but he can avoid

falling into their trap. This he does firstly by keeping his use of words down to the bare minimum, and secondly by choosing those words he does use very carefully. The warrior knows that all explanations and all descriptions are relative to his chosen frame of reference, but as all frames of reference are variables, he places no real importance upon explanations as such. For a warrior, an explanation is exactly what the word tells him it is, namely an *ex-plane-tion.* In order to be viewed more closely, what is being explained has quite literally been removed from its true plane, or been taken out of its true context. The moment anything is taken out of context, any information gathered about it must necessarily be impure, and in most cases downright inaccurate.

The only effective way in which to side-step the trap of words is through the practice of what is termed *not-doing* * . By refusing to accept words at their face value and by keeping in mind that words are mere symbols for the knowledge they veil, it is possible to use words safely. In truth, the only value words do have is to make us think more broadly, deeply, and further than before. Words are instruments with which we may assist others to probe the unknown and in this respect they are rightfully very important, but here their value stops. Moreover, it is vital to remember that the ability of words to reveal knowledge is dependent upon the listener's *proficiency* in the use of words, and relative to his *understanding* of their value.

What then should man's approach be to the use of words? This question has already been answered to a great extent by what has been stated so far, but one further point will clarify the issue quite well.

---

* *The act of choosing an opposite or different course to the one which would normally have been chosen. This practice is explained more fully in Chapter 9.*

A WARRIOR NEVER MAKES THE STUPID MISTAKE OF ASSUMING THAT THE WORLD IS ONLY WHAT WORDS WOULD SEEM TO INDICATE. A WARRIOR LIVES BY CHALLENGE, AND FOR HIM WORDS ARE NO LESS AND NO MORE THAN YET ANOTHER CHALLENGE.

In order to recognise the challenge inherent in words, the warrior must listen impeccably to their sound, their context, and most important of all, their implications. The true value of words lies in their *implications* rather than in the absolute values they carry by virtue of definition. Generally a warrior is capable of *seeing* the true knowledge veiled by the words a man has used, not so much from the actual words, but rather from their implications. More often than not an even deeper meaning can be extracted from the words the speaker has not used, namely the issues he has either consciously or unconsciously skirted.

By training himself to read between the lines and to listen to the unspoken message contained within a man's speech, the warrior begins to *see*. It must be explained here that essentially there is nothing visual in *seeing*; it is instead a direct flow of knowledge between orator and listener and even between object and observer. Seers explain this in terms of the alignment of energy fields, which technically speaking is correct, but it starts in the warrior's recognition of the fact that words were only invented to serve as instruments of communication. Initially words were quite harmless, then they became the means to define a mutually acceptable view of the world, and finally they have become the means whereby one man may dominate another, or even a whole nation of people. No seer, however, can ever be dominated by words, and much less be held prisoner within a fixed frame of reference or view of the world.

All seers start off in the same way. By aiming to break the fixation of their perception, trainee seers start off by questioning everything and anything, not in the sense of whether it is true or not, but in the sense of trying to fathom what it is they have *not* noticed. This is the only real difference between a scientist and a seer, yet the respective results of their research are remarkably different.

The scientist tries to prove everything according to a fixed frame of reference and therefore comes up with results which either prove things to be correct or incorrect, true or false. The seer, on the other hand, does not try to prove anything, but instead tries to find a way in which he may *use* what he has witnessed.

Because the scientist has to uphold absolute values, it is imperative for him to prove his knowledge according to his fixed frame of reference. The seer, acknowledging a fluid universe in which absolute values have no meaning, seeks only to use the forces of the universe without bothering to explain them. The seer knows that explanations are relevant only to the chosen frame of reference and thus have no effect upon the forces he is striving to use.

In this respect, the use of imagination is an excellent example. No orthodox scientist will ever lay himself open to being accused of imagining things. The seer, on the other hand, cares nothing for his image and therefore strives only to work out how best he may use this most magical property of the human mind.

The 'scientific intellectual' will agonize for days and years trying either to prove or disprove his theories. In total contrast, the seer does not care about such proofs, because the only proof he requires is whether or not his theory works. No-one today, neither scientist nor seer, can prove the existence of the assemblage point, but by working with it, and by moving it, the seer can do things the scientist cannot do. To the seer this *use* of the assemblage point is proof enough that it is tangible, real and capable of manipulation. From a scientific point of view, the assemblage point could well be described as a mere figment of the seer's imagination, but not so the effects of using it!

The ultimate difference between the scientist and the seer lies in their respective attitudes towards man and the world. To most scientists everything unknown can at some stage be explained in terms of a fixed frame of reference, through the use of words, formulas and theories. Generally, scientists see both man and the world as being fixed within a system of absolute values, even if this system is not fully understood. Thus, for the scientist, man and the world are merely intellectual exercises.

For the seer, on the contrary, man and the world are the most amazing confluence of ever-fluctuating permutations – an astonishing miracle of order flowing out of what can only be described as chaos. To the seer, both man and the world are the most marvellous mysteries which he knows he will never truly grasp, since understanding is based upon a fixed frame of reference, and the kaleidoscopic permutations and combinations that bring about constant motion, change and fluidity do not lend themselves to logic.

The scientist sees in words his hope of being able to reduce both man and the universe to a known intellectual formula. The seer finds in words or, more accurately, in the implications inherent within them, an opportunity for expressing his awe at the astonishing mystery and scope of both man and the universe. The difference between scientist and seer is staggering in its effects. The scientist leads man into a sterile life of ever-increasing boredom; the seer reminds man of his unlimited heritage as a magical being of an exciting and unknowable universe.

In man's fear of the unknown he has unwittingly, but nevertheless wilfully, traded excitement for boredom, adventure for security. In this respect words are a perfect testimony to this fact. Man would much rather adhere to the absolute and known value of words than chance the unknown by questioning the validity of their face value.

The warrior, who is first and foremost a free being, and secondly an adventurer and pioneer at heart, seeks always the hidden challenge and the mystery concealed by the face value of words. In his heart of hearts he feels, senses and simply knows that every word holds hidden within it the clue to a mystery. Therefore the warrior pays the most careful attention to words, turning them over and over in his mind, this way and that, searching out all of their possible implications. For a warrior to take words at their face value is to walk straight into the trap of ignorance and boredom – something which for him is a meaningless and stupid waste of time and energy.

Everything stated thus far relates to the Toltec view on the use of words. However, it is not only Toltecs who understand words in this manner. The following is a selection of quotations from the writings of some of the world's finest authors and poets, showing how each of these masters uses words in his own peculiar style. The writers selected are those who use words in a way which closely resembles the Toltec view. In this respect the quotations will assist the reader in becoming more familiar with the way in which words should be approached if they are to convey the truth they veil.

Throughout the following section the reader should try to spot the two different avenues of approach used by the writers, as an exercise in figuratively learning to read between the lines.

These two avenues will be defined and discussed in greater depth later on, but let it suffice for now to say that all people quite naturally fall into two distinct types, differentiated by Toltecs as *dreamers* and *stalkers.*

The dreamer has a somewhat serious approach, bringing the accent to bear on the good, the beautiful and the mysterious. On the other hand, the stalker is much more jovial, at times almost glib, and lays the accent on truth, paradox, satire and sometimes even rather caustic humour. Both types demand of their readers an intelligent and wide-awake approach, as none of these writings can be taken at face value, since every word and every phrase contains messages within messages.

Johann Wolfgang von Goethe gave excellent advice on the use of words when he said:

'The deed is everything, its repute nothing.' [2]

In this simple statement the author iterates the truth that no matter how impressive a man's words may be, unless they are substantiated by real action, they remain empty words. Actions always speak louder than words. He also stated that:

'All theory, dear friend, is grey, but the golden tree of actual life springs ever green.' [3]

Ralph Waldo Emerson said:

'Tis the good reader that makes the good book,' [4]

pointing out clearly the importance of the reader's proficiency in the handling of words, but he also states elsewhere:

> *'Converse with a mind that is grandly simple, and literature looks like word-catching.'* [5]

Emerson shows with this last sentence that he is well aware that it is the content of a person's words which is more important than the words themselves. William Blake echoes this in his verse:

> *'To see a World in a Grain of Sand,*
> *And a Heaven in a Wild Flower,*
> *Hold Infinity in the palm of your hand,*
> *And Eternity in an hour.'* [6]

These words are a beautiful example of *a mind that is grandly simple*, but they are also so much more. Contained in the first two lines is the concept that the world is not what it appears to be. Toltecs teach that the little things in life which are so often overlooked as being of no significance are just as important as anything else. Thus for the warrior, a grain of sand is infinitely more than just a grain of sand, and a wild flower reveals to him a wealth of knowledge.

Likewise, the last two lines of Blake's stanza are not merely pretty poetic words, but statements of great value. To *'hold Infinity in the palm of your hand'* is an allusion to the godlike potential of man. Man in his true essence is an infinite being who holds the unfoldment of his destiny, and therefore his potential, within his own hands. The last line, '*and Eternity in an hour*' is a scientific law as true as any of the laws currently upheld by orthodox science. In this one short phrase Blake indicates that law which Toltecs term the *compression of time.*

Albert Einstein proved mathematically that time is a dimension in its own right, something which Toltecs have understood and practised for a very long time. Yet science still does not grasp fully the subtle implications of this law. Put quite simply, time is inversely proportional to awareness. Mathematically it can be represented in the following equation:

*If **t** is the time taken to complete a task, and **a** is the degree of awareness involved, then:*

$$t = \frac{c}{a} \quad \text{where } c \text{ is a constant (time)}$$

*Therefore, as **a** tends to infinity, **t** tends to zero:*

$$0 = \frac{c}{\infty}$$

What this law means in practice is that the greater the degree of awareness, the less time is needed in order to understand a concept or to complete a task. This is what is meant by a *warrior compresses time.*

In continuing with our analysis of words, Henry David Thoreau explained that:

'It takes two to tell the truth – one to tell it, the other to hear it.' [1]

This is a very pointed statement on the importance not only of using words intelligently, but also of having to absorb them with discrimination.

As if to stress the fact that words ever veil the truth, Oscar Wilde said:

'The truth is rarely pure, and never simple.' [7]

Jonathan Swift, however, added that when words are properly used they are indeed the mark of an impeccable stalker. He says:

'Proper words in proper places, make the true definition of a style.' [8]

As if to prove Swift's point, Stephen Spender wrote the following two stanzas – stunning statements using the technique of a true stalker:

'I think continually of those who were truly great -
The names of those who in their lives fought for life,
Who wore at their hearts the fire's centre.'

'Born of the sun they travelled a short while towards the sun,
And left the vivid air signed with their honour.' [9]

Here Spender speaks volumes upon the origin of man, the concept of reincarnation, and upon the work of Toltecs throughout the ages. The true essence of these stanzas, however, exceeds the scope of this book; they have been included here merely to illustrate the technique of stalking as used within the medium of words.

Like anything else in the universe, words in themselves are neither good nor bad, but will always reflect our intent. In this, words can convey confusion, boredom and mental sterility; or they can convey beauty, mystery and the ineffable truth. The strange paradox of words is that language was born from the *mind* of man and yet its roots lie within the *heart* of man. As is the case with all paradoxes, if one is to answer the riddle of the sphinx, one has to use both mind and heart to circumvent the sphinx's lethal trap. In this respect Bernard Shaw stated:

'The man who listens to Reason is lost: Reason enslaves all whose minds are not strong enough to master her.' [10]

As if having anticipated that this statement would evoke question, Shaw clarifies it elsewhere in his writings:

'The reasonable man adapts himself to the world; the unreasonable man persists in trying to adapt the world to himself. Therefore all progress depends on the unreasonable man.' [11]

Again this is a masterful bit of stalking which brings home a wonderful piece of wisdom. Continuing in the same vein, the inimitable Shaw concludes:

'A man of great common sense and good taste – meaning thereby a man without originality or moral courage.' [12]

In the sentence above, Shaw cuttingly points out the debilitating effects of social conditioning and the mediocrity born of reason. In his own quiet way Blaise Pascal adds:

'The heart has its reasons which reason knows nothing of.' [13]

Echoing the value of the heart's own knowledge, Emerson's advice to man is:

'Hitch your wagon to a star.' [14]

Then, bringing home the point that all true knowledge lies within the heart, he says:

'Though we travel the world over to find the beautiful, we must carry it with us or we find it not.' [15]

In the following short verse, Blake amplifies this concept by stressing the futility of making a grab for things outside ourselves in an attempt to find happiness or, for that matter, knowledge:

'He who bends to himself a Joy
Doth the winged life destroy;
But he who kisses the Joy as it flies
Lives in Eternity's sunrise.' [16]

All in all, when it comes to using words, the approach of the warrior is clearly summed up in the words of Walt Whitman:

'Behold, I do not give lectures or a little charity, when I give I give myself.' [17]

In this respect the warrior uses the same yardstick with which to measure the potential in the words of others. As an apprentice once so aptly expressed it:

'Some people are so sincerely wrong.'

Oscar Wilde expressed the above opinion in this way:

'A little sincerity is a dangerous thing, and a great deal of it is absolutely fatal.' [18]

After reflecting on the different examples above, it is hoped that the reader will now better be able to grasp the fact that the warrior must, and does, approach words like any other challenge in his life. To take words for granted, or to use them in a helter-skelter fashion, is utter foolishness. Christ said:

'Not that which goeth into the mouth defileth a man; but that which cometh out of the mouth, this defileth a man.' [19]

A warrior takes careful note of this, firstly in his own speech, and secondly, in the words of others. It should always be remembered that a man is what his words reveal, provided that the listener has the ears to hear and does not get hooked on the face value of words.

All of the above has been an attempt to illustrate both the folly and the power of words, the falsehood and the truth, and especially the humour. Words are powerful tools in the hands of the warrior who has seen in them not only the challenge, but also the responsibility they bring.

Generally speaking, man has little regard for words. All over the world today people are demanding, amongst many other things, freedom of speech. Yet at the same time people often refuse to accept the responsibility that words bring. In this respect one can but laugh with Oscar Wilde when he says:

> *'Democracy means simply the bludgeoning of the people by the people for the people.'* [20]

It is easy enough to talk, and just as easy to talk with a great deal of conviction. People get so carried away by their own speeches, or by the speeches of others, that they will even get themselves killed for those utterances. But as William Thackeray put it so very aptly:

> *'Tis not the dying for a faith that is so hard, Master Harry – every man of every nation has done that – 'tis the living up to it that is difficult.'* [21]

Man will say anything that sounds good, and as he speaks so he believes – such is the power of the spoken word; it is in truth a commitment. In this respect the warrior heeds the advice of Goethe:

'Genius develops in quiet places,
Character out in the full current of human life.' [22]

Silence, inner and outer, is the gateway to true knowledge, whilst the masterful use of words, both in talking and in listening, is the gateway to freedom. Silence and words are but the two sides of the same coin, namely communication – the unspoken word often conveying even more than that spoken.

Finally, it should be realised that in his use of words the warrior is really in search of knowledge. The acquisition of such knowledge, however, requires skill.

THE SKILL OF THE WARRIOR LIES IN HIS ABILITY TO RECONCILE FEAR AND AWE.

The only way in which a warrior can develop this skill is for him to adopt a healthy sense of humour. An author who understood this to perfection was Oscar Wilde, who commented:

'We are all in the gutter, but some of us are looking at the stars.' [23]

This observation of Wilde's describes beautifully the humour, the folly, the unbending intent and the attitude of the warrior. It has been said that tears cleanse the soul, and true as this is, in the life of a warrior this cleansing is not enough. It is also vital for the well-being of the warrior to be able to laugh, because this laughter brings him temporary relief from the pressure of the battle he fights day in and day out. In this regard Goethe understood full well what it entails to be a warrior, for he writes:

'You must either conquer and rule or lose and serve, suffer or triumph, and be the anvil or the hammer.' [24]

As far as folly is concerned, Shaw was a man who possessed a keen sense of wit, and who could also laugh at himself, as when he said:

'I never resist temptation, because I have found that things that are bad for me do not tempt me.' [25]

The folly of our own actions constantly provides us with an inexhaustible source of laughter. Edgar Allan Poe expressed the concept of folly so very eloquently:

'All that we see or seem
Is but a dream within a dream.' [26]

In these two short lines Poe sums up most graphically the Toltec attitude towards man's normal perception of his world. Man sees and experiences the world according to his frame of reference but, if the assemblage point is shifted far enough, a totally new and different world is assembled which is every bit as real and objective as the one man normally perceives. Under the impact of such an act all our endeavours in daily life amount to nothing more than folly.

The greatest author of all, William Shakespeare, expressed folly in this way:

'Our revels now are ended. These our actors,
As I foretold you, were all spirits and
Are melted into air, into thin air:
And, like the baseless fabric of this vision,
The cloud-capp'd towers, the gorgeous palaces,
The solemn temples, the great globe itself,
Yea, all which it inherit, shall dissolve
And, like the insubstantial pageant faded,
Leave not a rack behind. We are such stuff
As dreams are made of, and our little life

Is rounded with a sleep.' [27]

To these words of Shakespeare Frank Herbert adds the poignant statement:

'I think what a joy it is to be alive, and I wonder if I'll ever leap inward to the root of this flesh and know myself as once I was. The root is there. Whether any act of mine can find it, that remains tangled in the future. But all things a man can do are mine. Any act of mine may do it.' [28]

This is a most apt description of the mood of a warrior. It shows the way in which he views himself and his task in life, that is, to try to unravel the mystery of his true being. On a quieter note of almost reverential awe, Herbert, like the warrior, concludes:

'There exists no separation between gods and men; one blends softly casual into the other.' [29]

Perhaps, in the final analysis, no-one has ever expressed the mood of a warrior better than Herman Hesse when he wrote:

'I learned through my body and soul that it was necessary for me to sin, that I needed lust, that I had to strive for property, and experience nausea and the depths of despair in order to learn not to resist them, in order to love the world, and no longer compare it with some kind of desired imaginary world, some imaginary vision of perfection, but to leave it as it is, to love it and be glad to belong to it. This stone is a stone; it is also animal, God and Buddha. I do not respect and love it because it was one thing and will become something else, but because it has already long

been everything and always is everything. I love it just because it is a stone, because today and now it appears to me a stone.' [30]

Such is the mood of a warrior; such is the impeccability of his spirit. This is his challenge. Words, spoken and written, are a part of that challenge.

TIGER

No man can be trapped without his consent.

(Pencil drawing: Susan Emily)

Susan Emily

CHAPTER THREE

TAKING THE GAP TO FREEDOM

THE ONLY FAILURE IN LIFE IS THE FAILURE TO FIGHT.

When one looks at the lives lived by average men and women today one is invariably struck by the oppressively boring and humdrum existence they are in a sense forced to lead. Average man is born, grows up, goes to school, perhaps even to college or university, finds himself a job, a wife, starts a family, saves for a car, a house and furniture, goes on his annual vacation, grows old and finally dies. One cannot help but wonder how a man manages to remain sane and even reasonably content under such severe conditions of boredom. Yet this is the lot of the majority of mankind today.

At some point in their lives at least some of these people ask themselves the question: 'Is this all there is to life?' However, they seldom come up with an answer to their quandary. Sadly, unable to find a reasonable and practical solution, they feel forced to resign themselves to their lot, making the best of what they have.

> *LIFE FOR AVERAGE MAN IS A RATHER VAGUE AND MONOTONOUS AFFAIR – AN EXISTENCE WHICH IS NOT COMPLETELY DEVOID OF AMUSEMENT, BUT ONE IN WHICH HE LISTLESSLY WANDERS FROM ONE TYPE OF ACTIVITY TO THE NEXT, ONLY TO FIND THAT THE HAPPINESS HE IS SEEKING IS CONSTANTLY ELUDING HIM. THE LIFE OF SUCH A MAN BECOMES FILLED WITH A SENSE OF EMPTINESS AND A*

DULL LONGING TO HAVE THAT EMPTINESS FILLED, BUT NOT KNOWING WHAT IT IS HE SEEKS, THE MAN DISCOVERS INSTEAD A NUMBING SENSE OF FUTILITY CREEPING INTO HIS HEART. THEN ALL TOO SOON HE FINDS HIS LIFE HAS SLIPPED THROUGH HIS FINGERS, SPENT ON THE MEANINGLESS TRIVIALITIES OF HUMAN PETTINESS.

We all start off life as average men and women, but this does not mean that we do not have the ability to mould our lives according to our choice. We may feel as if we are the victims of fate, and although it is true that no man can escape his destiny, we all have the capacity to rise above fate if we so choose. We are all given the opportunity at some point in our lives to decide for ourselves what we would like out of life.

THE PROBLEM IS THAT WE ARE ALL BORN FOOLS, FOR SUCH IS OUR HUMAN CONDITION.

In our foolishness we take great pride in ourselves for being human. Consequently we demand for ourselves certain privileges and rights, and then we make a huge fuss and become very upset if our demands are not met. Yet, look closely at man. Look at what he does to the planet, to his fellow men, and to the other creatures who share the planet with him. Look at man's secret emotions and his hidden thoughts. People have a great deal to say about ethics and morality, yet they carefully conceal feelings and thoughts that are often so vile and poisonous that they cause a psychic pollution which is even more destructive than physical pollution.

MAN REGARDS HIMSELF AS BEING BETTER THAN AN ANIMAL – BUT MOSTLY HE LIVES AN EXISTENCE WHICH IS WORSE THAN THAT OF ANIMALS.

If we live such lives, is it at all surprising that we end up feeling like victims? Mostly we live the lives we do because we fear that not to do so would be madness.

UNFORTUNATELY ALL OF US ARE ALREADY MAD.

Take a closer look at man and compare your plight with his. Can you deviate from what you have grown up to believe is right – from what you have been taught is right? Can you? The answer is, 'No'.

PEOPLE ARE KEPT IN PSYCHIC BONDAGE THROUGH THEIR SOCIAL CONDITIONING. TO KEEP A MAN IN PHYSICAL BONDAGE IS AN ACT OF SLAVERY; TO KEEP HIM IN PSYCHIC BONDAGE IS A HEINOUS ACT OF BLACK MAGIC. YET SINCE ALL OF MANKIND IS AFFLICTED BY THIS EVIL, ALL MEN PARTICIPATE IN IT. MAN PERPETUATES THIS VILE PRACTICE BY INFLICTING IT UPON HIS OWN CHILDREN. THUS IT IS THAT THE ACTIONS OF EVERY MAN ARE CONSTANTLY BEING DEFINED BY THE DEBILITATING MEDIOCRITY BORN OF SOCIAL CONDITIONING.

We can of course always rationalize our behaviour in order to feel better about it. For example, as parents we can argue that our actions are naturally the best for our children. It is after all our duty as parents to guide our young ones in the right direction. Sadly, and far too often, we consider ourselves good parents when we impose our will, our ideas and beliefs upon our children. Then once we have successfully brainwashed them into behaving, feeling, and even thinking like us, we bask in the self-satisfaction of knowing that we have given the world dutiful citizens who will meekly tow the line.

Such justifications change nothing. To guide our children with love and firmness is one thing, but to force our will upon them is to abuse our privilege as parents. To encourage our children to think for themselves and to take responsibility for their own actions is our duty. On the other hand, to break their will by forcing them to surrender to our judgement is an unforgivable infringement of human rights.

Children need love, care and firm guidance, but they also need understanding, and above all, respect. If we never listen to our children we cannot be surprised if they stop listening to us. If we merely listen so as to frustrate them at every turn then we have no right to feel hurt if one day they turn upon us in anger and bitterness. Children learn far more from the example set for them than from speeches. If we listen to their questions, their requests and their wishes with respect and understanding then they too will listen to our advice and guidance with the same respect and understanding. If we love our children without turning that love into a ball and chain, our children will always embrace us with that same love.

What is true for us as parents is equally true for us as citizens of the world. All of us have had to suffer the atrocities of social conditioning, yet it should also be realised that in reality there are no victims.

NO MAN CAN BE TRAPPED WITHOUT HIS CONSENT.

No-one can enslave a person against his will. Bearing out this point are the many people in the world who have fought against and broken away from all conventional behaviour and discipline. It is only regrettable that although such people have had enough *personal power* to break free, they often do not have sufficient *power* to define for themselves a new purpose and a new direction in life.

Without purpose and direction such people frequently end up on the wrong side of the law – a law made by average men for living an average existence. Having broken away from the traditions and customs of this law, such rebels find little sympathy under a law enforced by those from whom they tried to escape in the first place.

If these rebels are unable to find a new purpose in life but are nevertheless clever enough to stay on the right side of the law, they invariably become what are known to Toltecs as *petty tyrants.* Petty tyrants spend their lives giving vent to their inner rage and frustration by making the lives of everyone around them a total misery. These people will often inflict upon their own children the very crimes their parents inflicted upon them.

In view of what has been stated this far, ask yourself what you are. Where do you fit into the scenario of life? Be honest with yourself in this. Do not fool yourself by immediately assuming that you are unique, for none of us stands in isolation to life. Are you a conspirator in black magic? Are you perhaps a petty tyrant? In order to answer these questions, think of the people in your life. Do they respect you? Do they truly love you? Do they trust you?

People are always the mirrors in which we see our own reflection. But these mirrors also show us our prejudices. If some reflect love and others reflect anger, then we can see whom we love, and whom we treat with disdain. We are all inherently dishonest, but our mirrors never lie. Mirrors always show us exactly how we think, feel and act towards the world around us. We can deny a reflection as loudly and as vehemently as we like, but it will never change until we ourselves change. Once one has changed, then one's reflection must also change – such is the law of light and reflection.

However, a warrior will sometimes purposefully project an image specifically aimed at misleading others. This is what is known as *stalking*. There are several reasons why a warrior will stalk others, the most important of which is in dealing with a petty tyrant. Petty tyrants are never pleasant people to deal with; in short they make our lives a misery in one way or another, but by handling them correctly they can also bring us many gifts of knowledge.

A petty tyrant is much more than merely a mirror, because such a person also shows us our weaknesses. It is for this reason that a warrior will willingly encourage a petty tyrant to hound him. In order to do this a warrior has to bait the petty tyrant, but he also must change his ways quickly and efficiently so as to avoid falling into the clutches of the petty tyrant. This amounts to much the same thing as teasing a lion – it is not only tricky, but also highly dangerous. Yet if a petty tyrant is properly stalked, it teaches us much, and it forces us to bring out of ourselves potentials which otherwise we would not have known we possessed.

> *MAN'S ONLY JUSTIFICATION FOR PHYSICAL EXISTENCE IS TO LEARN; THIS IS HIS DESTINY WHICH HE CANNOT AVOID UNDER ANY CIRCUMSTANCES.*

Learning must be understood as meaning *experiential knowledge*, because the Warrior's Path is first and foremost a practical path. Gathering information is not true learning. Information is to all intents and purposes useless, unless it can be put to good practical use in one's daily life, and the only knowledge which is of value is that which enables a man to better understand his destiny so that he can aid in its unfoldment. Hard as this may be to accept for those who believe that they control their lives, it is nevertheless true.

Man has been debating the question of free choice for ages, but he still stubbornly refuses to acknowledge that he has only two choices; either to aid in the unfoldment of his destiny, or to frustrate that unfoldment. If he follows his destiny he leads a happy and prosperous life; if on the other hand he frustrates his destiny he experiences hardship and misery.

It is incomprehensible that any man should wilfully prevent his destiny from unfolding. Nonetheless, this is exactly what man so often does, albeit unconsciously, and purely because he is caught up in the momentum of his social conditioning. Social conditioning does not allow for the unfoldment of anything other than what is expected of us from our fellow men.

It should be realised, however, that social conditioning is of course dependent upon a mutually-accepted universal view of the world. Such a commonly-accepted view entails that everyone must have the same frame of reference as everybody else. This automatically excludes all views, ideas and feelings which do not conform to mankind's common point of view. Yet man was never destined to be confined to only one point of view.

MAN'S DESTINY IS TO LEARN BY EXPERIENCING ALL OF THE COUNTLESS POSSIBLE MANIFESTATIONS OF LIFE CONTAINED WITHIN THE UNIVERSE.

It is perfectly possible to move the assemblage point from its normal position and thereby to bring about a totally new view of the world. What precludes mankind from doing this is mostly the lack of the necessary knowledge. Admittedly this knowledge has not always been freely available, but even when it is, it should be understood that there are no gifts as such in this world. We end up by having to pay in one way or another for everything we receive – even so-called gifts.

IN THIS UNIVERSE NOTHING IS FOR NOTHING; ALL KNOWLEDGE MUST BE EARNED AT GREAT COST.

THE COST OF TRUE KNOWLEDGE IS ONE'S LIFE. THE KNOWLEDGE YOU SEEK CAN ONLY BE ACQUIRED BY DEDICATING YOUR LIFE TO IT.

YOU CANNOT WALK THE PATH OF KNOWLEDGE WITHOUT LIVING THAT KNOWLEDGE; THEREFORE YOUR COMMITMENT MUST BE ABSOLUTE.

WALKING THE PATH OF KNOWLEDGE DOES NOT COME NATURALLY TO MAN; THEREFORE ALL LEARNING IS FORCED.

Most people would like to have knowledge, but would prefer it if they could simply purchase it from somewhere rather than having to work for it. This is one of the reasons why today there are so many schools offering enlightenment and why it is not too difficult to find those gurus who will, for a price, shoulder your responsibility to learn. But as has already been pointed out, true knowledge is knowledge of the self, and such knowledge cannot be given to us by anyone, nor can it be bought for any money in the world.

The only thing the true spiritual teacher can give his students is the necessary guidance to enable them to tap their own hidden resources. To do this, the spiritual teacher must force his students into learning who and what they truly are, for without this knowledge there can be no tapping of one's potential. However, to face ourselves, to take stock of who we are, and to acknowledge even our shortcomings, is never pleasant and is most of the time very frightening.

In view of this, it is not surprising that a lot of people seek out only those teachers who make them feel good and who promise to do the work for them. The true spiritual teacher is never comfortable to be with, for he invariably challenges us to look at aspects of ourselves which we spend our lives trying to hide from everybody, including ourselves. Such a teacher does not care what his students may think of him, or whether they like him or not, because his only concern is to see that they get that knowledge which they are seeking, and for which they came to him. Obviously teachers such as these are few and difficult to find, simply because it is the rare man indeed who will put his reputation at stake, and who is prepared to love his students more than his desire for recognition.

KNOWLEDGE IS EVER GREATER AND MORE POWERFUL THAN MAN. TO WALK THE PATH OF KNOWLEDGE IS TO FIGHT FOR SURVIVAL; THEREFORE IF YOU COME TO THIS PATH TO LEARN, THEN YOU MUST BE PREPARED TO FIGHT

AS IF YOUR LIFE DEPENDS UPON IT.

IN THE BEGINNING, NO MAN EVER KNOWS WHAT IS ENTAILED IN LEARNING BECAUSE HE DOES NOT KNOW WHAT IT IS TO BE A MAN. THUS HE DESIRES REWARDS WHICH ARE MOSTLY IN CONFLICT WITH HIS DESTINY AND WHICH THEREFORE CANNOT BE MATERIALIZED.

Generally, people are enthralled by stories of the so-called supernatural, of heroes and marvellous deeds requiring genius. In hearing or reading these stories every man, woman and child secretly, deep down inside, sees him or herself as the hero of the story and they begin to wonder what they would do if they had been a genius or someone with supernatural powers. Yet in thinking like this, these people do not really believe they are capable of such deeds, and in most cases they would be highly embarrassed at having to disclose their secret dreams.

Social conditioning is such that it does not allow for ordinary people to do the extraordinary. Heroes and heroines are only allowed if they are placed firmly outside the parameters defined by social conditioning. It is acceptable for a sorcerer to perform magic, because sorcerers exist outside the confines of normal people, but for a secretary suddenly to exhibit magical powers within her office environment is somehow considered a serious violation of social custom. In their fear of being ostracised or of being regarded as abnormal, people desperately adhere to the limits of social conformity. Thus the only thing left for them is to indulge occasionally in secret dreams.

In these secret dreams men and women mould their lives and, depending on the extent to which they believe their dreams are possible, they unconsciously begin to project their inner wishes, hopes and fears onto the world around them. If the person concerned experiences a lot of inner anger, then he eventually begins to see that anger in the world around him. For that person, everybody apparently begins to take on an aggressive attitude. Likewise, if the person experiences inner fear, the world around him becomes ever more menacing and frightening.

In reality, people rarely dream of only one thing, but rather of a whole mixture of conflicting ideas. Hence their lives become that same strange mixture of feelings and thoughts. This accounts for the fact that a person's actions can often be contradictory. We see that in one particular type of incident a man can act like a true hero, and yet in another situation he can behave like a total coward.

It is important to realise that a great percentage of a person's secret dreams hardly ever surface into the light of full awareness. Instead, they are kept at bay in the shadowy world of semiconscious emotional impulses, usually through an overpowering sense of guilt. Here in the shadow world these dreams are fed by a lush crop of suppressed emotions and desires. Breeding most prolifically, these dreams produce all manner of strangely distorted ideas and hopes which man considers to be his life's ambition and a reflection of his true self.

In the light of all this it is not surprising that man does not know who and what he really is, or what his real wishes and thoughts ought to be. Therefore no-one ever comes to the Path of Knowledge with the right expectations or, for that matter, with the correct motives.

The best that any novice to the Path of Knowledge can do is to come with an open mind, prepared to do whatever it takes to uncover the true nature of knowledge and, more important still, the true nature of his being. Only then can there be any real progress. Only when the seeker begins to delve into those parts of himself which he has confined to the dark regions of semiconsciousness does he understand how utterly frightening knowledge can be; hence the necessity of coming prepared to fight and struggle as if one's life depended on the outcome.

LEARNING ABOUT THE INNER SELF IS NOT ONLY

FRIGHTENING, BUT IS ALSO THE MOST CONSUMING OF ALL POSSIBLE PURSUITS.

TO APPROACH KNOWLEDGE IS AKIN TO ENTERING INTO A BATTLE FOR ONE'S LIFE. HENCE THE WARRIOR APPROACHES KNOWLEDGE WITH FULL ALERTNESS, WITH FEAR, WITH RESPECT AND WITH ABSOLUTE ASSURANCE. ANY MAN FOOLISH ENOUGH NOT TO APPROACH KNOWLEDGE IN THIS WAY WILL REGRET HIS ERROR BITTERLY. ON THE OTHER HAND, IF HE IS WISE ENOUGH TO ACKNOWLEDGE HIS SEARCH FOR KNOWLEDGE AS BEING A MATTER OF LIFE AND DEATH HE WILL HAVE NO CAUSE FOR REGRETS, FOR SUCH AN APPROACH CANCELS OUT THE CARELESS ACTIONS OF THE FOOL.

The aphorism above is known as *the shield of a warrior* and it warrants some careful analysis. A full analysis will be given in the following chapter, but it has been included here to bring home the fact that any approach to knowledge is a most serious action for which the seeker must take full responsibility. To approach knowledge casually or flippantly is a grave mistake, because once something has been learned it can never again be unlearned. Information can be gathered quickly, and forgotten just as quickly, but not so true knowledge of the self.

Generally, man never comes to grips with true knowledge, mainly because he does not really know what it is he is seeking. Most people live entirely within the light reflected off the surface of their awareness and, as a result, they never plumb the dark depths of that awareness, and so are never whole as human beings.

However, to have real knowledge, and the power with which to utilize that knowledge, a person must be whole. He must know every part of himself intimately. He must bring every potential, for good or bad, into the light of his full awareness, no matter how frightening or unpleasant these dark areas of himself may appear to be. It is for this reason that every apprentice to the

Warrior's Path is taught the technique known as *recapitulation.*

From the very first day of his training every apprentice is expected to begin recapitulating his entire life in minute detail, from the present moment right back to the moment of birth. This is obviously not an easy task, nor is it quickly accomplished. In the majority of cases a total recall takes many years, but it must be followed through and done properly if the apprentice is ever going to succeed upon the Path of Knowledge. Only through the recapitulation of his entire life can the apprentice truly understand his total being. This technique is explained in detail in Chapter 8.

In what has been stated so far the quality and nature of knowledge should be reasonably clear.

> *TRUE KNOWLEDGE IS TO EXPERIENCE THE INNER SELF; BUT SINCE THE INNER BEING IS UNIQUE TO EVERY INDIVIDUAL, KNOWLEDGE CANNOT BE ASSIMILATED BY TALKING ABOUT IT.*

> *KNOWLEDGE GAINED FROM SOMEONE ELSE LACKS THE CONFIDENCE NECESSARY TO IMPLEMENT THAT KNOWLEDGE. CONFIDENCE IS CULTIVATED ONLY THROUGH PRACTICE.*

No man can trade upon the knowledge of another person, simply because the only knowledge which we can use with certainty is that knowledge which we have acquired through personal experience. Any person can read the theory entailed in walking a tightrope, but such theory will not keep him from falling off should he try to walk a rope. Only through repeated practice, and through trial and error, does he finally manage to walk on the rope without falling off.

On a more subtle note, we see that it does not help to be told you are beautiful when you consider yourself to be ugly. Only when you yourself believe that you are good-looking will you accept compliments on your appearance, but the only way in which to believe in your good looks is to practise believing that you are beautiful. It has been said that *'beauty is in the eye of the beholder'*, but although this old adage is used glibly by most people, they do not really believe it. Yet, what is beautiful to one person is often very unattractive to someone else. For example, there are men who find women with voluptuous breasts highly appealing, but there are also some men who prefer women with small, well-rounded breasts. Nonetheless, in both cases neither of these two types of women will see themselves as being attractive, unless they themselves believe it and practise being confident in their charm.

Both of these examples are true for every situation in our lives, but here again we so often encounter the devastating effects of social conditioning. If a child is clumsy in learning to walk he is repeatedly told that he is clumsy. As an adult he continues to be told how very clumsy and awkward he was as a baby. Such a person will end up believing that something like walking a tightrope is totally beyond him. Likewise, if the current fashion in magazines is for women with large breasts, women with small breasts feel inadequately endowed, but if the fashion happens to be for flat-chested ladies, women with big breasts desperately try to conceal their assets.

The first task given to every apprentice is systematically to start undoing all of his social conditioning, for whilst he is still firmly in the grips of this conditioning he cannot make any real progress. The technique for accomplishing this is called *not-doing,* and this is practised in conjunction with *recapitulation.* This technique will be explained fully in Chapter 9.

In the same way that a total recall of a person's entire life takes a long time to complete, so too is social conditioning not undone overnight. The apprentice will not immediately succeed in undoing anything of real significance, but by systematically working at it he gradually begins to wear away at that conditioning bit by bit. It also often happens that the apprentice finds himself coming up against what seems to be an insurmountable barrier in either his recapitulation or his not-doing. He becomes stuck, as it were, and feels that no matter how hard he tries, he just does not seem capable of recalling anything of real value, nor does he seem to be able to execute not-doing.

> *WHEN THE WARRIOR FAILS IN ANY ONE PARTICULAR PURSUIT OF KNOWLEDGE HE IS NOT DEFEATED, BECAUSE IN WALKING THE PATH OF KNOWLEDGE WE FIGHT MANY BATTLES – SOME WE WIN, SOME WE LOSE. SUCCESS LIES NOT IN HOW MANY BATTLES WE HAVE WON, BUT IN HOW WELL WE HAVE FOUGHT.*

If the apprentice comes up against such an obstacle he has no other recourse but to continue struggling and trying to make a break-through. It may appear to him as if he is failing but this is not really true, because it is always only a temporary failure, if I may use such an odd phrase.

By continuing to struggle the apprentice forces himself to break the fixation of his assemblage point. This is important because we are incapable of any real progress until we can move the assemblage point. This is why the Old Seers always forcibly moved the assemblage points of their apprentices prior to instruction.

No-one spends his entire life with the assemblage point in exactly the same position as when he was born. Throughout life man is constantly adjusting his assemblage point unconsciously. However, in doing so, he 'forgets' many of his experiences and the means by which he has arrived at that knowledge.

To understand this it should be realised that the assemblage point is very much like the dial on a tuner. The purpose of such a dial is to enable us to access certain radio frequencies which give us a particular broadcasting station. Every time we move the dial we will access another band of frequencies which will of course constitute another station.

The assemblage point of man works in exactly the same way in that it gives us access to certain energy fields which constitute our view of the world. Under the impact of this view we gain certain experiences and knowledge which are peculiar only to that particular view. If then we access other energy fields we also access another view. This new view causes us to lose contact with or to 'forget' the experiences and knowledge gained previously. Needless to say, we do not really forget. It is just that our old view becomes overlaid with the impact of our new view and its attendant experiences.

When knowledge becomes overlaid in this manner it becomes what has been termed subliminal or subconscious. The fact that knowledge is subconscious does not imply that it ceases to influence our actions. On the contrary, our thoughts and feelings, and consequently also our actions, are continuously being influenced by this subconscious knowledge. This is why an apprentice will often struggle to break an old habit. Such subconscious knowledge has the tendency to pop up most unexpectedly, and the apprentice finds himself having concluded an act triggered by this subliminal knowledge even before he realises what he is doing.

It therefore stands to reason that in order to have total recall and also to be able successfully to practise not-doing, it is necessary to be able to move the assemblage point back to all of its former positions. Only by accessing these former positions can we recall the knowledge gained there, and the habits initiated by those experiences.

It is vital to grasp that it does not matter if at first we meet only with apparent failure. Paradoxical as it may sound, success in walking the Path of Knowledge does not lie in the outcome of our struggle, but only in how impeccably we struggle, because it is this struggle which forces us to move the assemblage point. Once we can move the assemblage point everything falls into place smoothly and effortlessly. The only thing which is a struggle is to make the assemblage point move in the first place. Once this has been accomplished the road lies clear ahead.

This struggle to move the assemblage point is the only thing of value in all of the instruction given to an apprentice. It does not matter which technique is used or what the task may entail; the only purpose of any instruction is to guide the apprentice into struggling to make his assemblage point fluid.

Also, the greater the struggle, the greater will be the apprentice's fluidity in the end. This is analogous to a weight-lifter in training; the more weights he has to push up, the greater will be his strength. Yet the effects of social conditioning are such that if at first a person tries and does not succeed, that person immediately assumes he has failed. Concluding from this that he does not have the necessary ability, such a person invariably gives up trying.

The important point here is to define what exactly constitutes so-called failure or success. This concept can only be understood in the context of what is meant by walking a particular path, irrespective of whether this path is a spiritual path or a career.

> *THE VALUE OF A PATH LIES IN HOW YOU WALK IT. IF YOU FEEL THAT THE PATH YOU ARE WALKING IS NOT FOR YOU, THEN YOU SHOULD ABANDON IT IMMEDIATELY. HOWEVER, YOUR DECISION TO WALK A PATH OR NOT SHOULD BE BASED ON THAT CLARITY WHICH SPRINGS FROM THE DISCIPLINED LIFE OF A WARRIOR, AND NOT ON FEAR OR AMBITION. DECISIONS TAKEN IN THE SOBER LIGHT OF CLARITY CANNOT POSSIBLY OFFEND ANYONE, LEAST OF ALL YOURSELF.*

As we have already seen, at the end of the day it does not matter how many battles we have won or how many we have lost, as the only thing of importance is whether or not we fought and, if we did, how well we fought. Did we run from a battle because of fear, or did we fight bravely, giving it our all?

No warrior will dispute that knowledge can sometimes be extremely frightening, especially that knowledge which brings our sense of security into jeopardy. The majority of people simply do not have the courage to fight a battle which they know is going to put their most treasured ideas and pet beliefs to the test. When challenged in this way most people will rather turn tail and flee than face the possibility that they may have to give up ideas which they have always held to be at the base of everything that is important to them. This fear of loss can be so overpowering that if a man is cornered into having to face such a battle he may even resort to suicide, rather than surrender.

To run from a path because you cannot face the battles it brings you is to be a coward. Likewise, to turn away from a path because it does not meet up with your initial expectations is utter foolishness. Neither of these options have any real clarity in them, for one is based on fear, while the other is based on assumption grounded in ambition. Fear and ambition both lack sobriety, and without sobriety failure will eventually supersede all further progress.

On the other hand, we sometimes also see that even when a man has come to realise that the path he is walking does not suit him, he will still continue with it merely because he lacks the courage to abandon it. For such a man to abandon the path means having to acknowledge to himself and to others that he has been wrong. The man sees this as an affront to himself and possibly even to those around him. In a case like this the man concerned, instead of admitting that he has been wrong, will begin to defend his path passionately, trying his best to justify his actions through rationalization.

CONSIDER EVERY PATH CAREFULLY, TESTING IT IN WHICHEVER WAY YOU FEEL NECESSARY – THEN ASK YOURSELF, BUT ONLY YOURSELF, ONE QUESTION: 'DOES THIS PATH HAVE A HEART?'
ANY PATH IS MUCH THE SAME AS ANY OTHER PATH. SOME PATHS WIND THIS WAY AND THAT – SOME PATHS GO STRAIGHT; BUT IN THE END NO PATH GOES ANYWHERE AT ALL. THE ONLY DIFFERENCE BETWEEN ONE PATH AND ANOTHER IS THAT SOME HAVE A HEART AND SOME DO NOT. THE PATH THAT HAS A HEART WILL UPLIFT YOU, EASE YOUR BURDEN AND BRING YOU JOY. THE PATH WITH NO HEART WILL MAKE YOU STUMBLE, IT WILL BREAK YOUR SPIRIT, AND FINALLY CAUSE YOU TO LOOK UPON YOUR LIFE WITH ANGER AND BITTERNESS.

Average man is hardly ever on a path with a heart, for most of the time he walks the path demarcated for him by his social conditioning. Most people hate so many things in their lives, be it their jobs, their cars, their houses, a certain relative, or a pet fear. Consequently they spend the greater portion of their lives feeling irritable and unhappy, often cursing their life at every turn and wishing it were different. One constantly hears from these people comments such as: 'If only I had better health. If only I had more money. If only my wife was more understanding and co-operative. If only my children would listen to me. If only the political situation in the country was not so threatening. If only I could change the past. If only I knew the future. If only...'

Such a man or woman never lives in the present moment, for they are always living either in the past or in the future. To such a person the present is irrelevant and of no consequence, because it is always superseded by the unhappy past, or by an uncertain future. This clearly is not a path with a heart, for it offers no peace and no joy, no sense of wonder and mystery; instead it offers only a desolate journey which is bleak and stark, uninteresting and thoroughly depressing.

If we lead such an oppressive life we have very little enthusiasm for fighting any sort of battle, for what is there in such a life worth fighting for? Slowly but surely a most debilitating feeling of unworthiness and inadequacy begins to take over. The person concerned becomes overwhelmed by a heavy sense of futility and finally capitulates, surrendering all will to continue fighting. This is tantamount to having failed. To stop trying is to be defeated.

The point is that in life there can be no failure as such. To lose one battle of the great many battles we have to fight throughout life is not failure – it is merely one battle lost. Even when we lose a battle, the thing that matters is what we have learned through that experience. Provided we fight impeccably we will learn, and it is this learning which is of value, not the outcome of the battle. The only failure in life is the failure to fight.

The warrior is a man who fights for his freedom from social conditioning; for his freedom to think and decide for himself; for his freedom to move his assemblage point at will and thereby access any view of the world he may choose; and above all, for his freedom to enjoy his life and the abundant experiences it brings him. To live one's life in this way does not mean that all one's desires are automatically fulfilled, for this depends upon one's destiny in a particular lifetime. But it does mean that one's destiny, whether it is to be wealthy and to live in a mansion, or whether it is to lead a humble life in a small home, will unfold peacefully and quietly. In that quietness of life one finds the joy and wonder which springs from knowing that one is walking a path with a heart, for the heart is ever where our true destiny lies.

Before we have come to know who we really are and what our true fate in this life is, we always have a great many wishes and desires which we believe will make us totally happy should they be fulfilled. But when our destiny finally unfolds we are always, without exception, struck by the beauty and wonder of it all. Even in our wildest imaginings we can never dream up anything even remotely as good and as exciting as our own true destiny.

> *THE WARRIOR IS A MAN WHO HAS LEARNED TO LOVE LIFE AND ALL THE MANY RICHNESSES IT BRINGS HIM — MOST OF ALL THE PATH WHERE HE WALKS. THERE IS FOR THE WARRIOR NO GREATER JOY THAN TO WALK A PATH WITH A HEART. ON THIS PATH HE WALKS, THRILLED BY THE WONDER OF IT ALL, AND IN HIS JOY HE GIVES THANKS IN HIS HEART FOR THIS MARVELLOUS PRIVILEGE BY EMBRACING EVERYTHING HE ENCOUNTERS WITH LOVE AND GRATITUDE.*

To lead the life of a warrior fighting for his freedom is to lead a life of success – success in the sense of walking a path with a heart, on which one's destiny unfolds in the most marvellous and joyful of ways. On this path every challenge the warrior encounters is for him yet another exciting battle, an adventure which he knows will lead him to even more undiscovered wonders in his life. Yet every warrior starts off life just like any other man or woman. The apprentice to the Warrior's Path has exactly the same fears and the same doubts as any other man; the only difference being that he has taken his courage into both hands and, having steeled himself, has taken the *gap to freedom*.

Once we have been brave enough to *seize our fleeting moment of chance*, one thing begins to lead to another until finally, one day, in the midst of a battle, we suddenly find that our command has indeed become the Eagle's command. From that moment on we are free beings, the world becomes our oyster and joy flows unimpeded without end.

This is the Eagle's gift to man – to all men who are willing to try, and to keep on trying whatever the cost. The reward though, is so much more, so very much more than the effort it takes to reach out for that gift.

BEAR

If you are not strong enough to fight, you have no choice but to accept the life of a slave. But the hunter is a free being who cannot submit himself to slavery; for him there is no choice but to fight. If then he dies in that fight, at least he will die as a free being, and not as a slave.
(Pencil drawing: Susan Emily)

CHAPTER FOUR

HUNTING FOR POWER

THE BEST HUNTERS ARE NOT THOSE WITH A NATURAL APTITUDE FOR HUNTING, BUT THOSE WHO HAVE HAD TO STRUGGLE LONG AND HARD TO LEARN EVERY TRICK OF THE TRADE.

Before we can tackle the concept of the *hunter* and what it means to *hunt power* we must first define the opponent. So the natural question is: 'What is *power*?'

It is not easy to define *power* without getting tied up in words. It will be remembered from the Truths of Awareness, that *power* is defined as being the *energy of alignment*, meaning that it is the force which is released when energy fields inside the cocoon become aligned with the corresponding energy fields outside the cocoon. The result of this alignment is perception. So we can also say that *power* is the *product of perception*.

These are the two traditional definitions of *power*, but in themselves they tell us very little about how we should interpret *power* in practice. We can no more see *power* than we can see perception, but we can witness the *effects* of both.

The effect of *power* is perhaps best described as being what we understand as *vitality,* or alternatively, *energy.* If you feel inspired by watching the sunrise, that enthusiasm you experience is the effect of *power*, or the effect of having perceived. The enthusiasm or vitality is not *power* per se, but rather the effect of *power*, or more accurately, *personal power**.

From these definitions it stands to reason that if the assemblage point is firmly fixed in one position then perception is also fixed. This means that we perceive everything according to that particular *frame of reference*, termed a *view of the world*. Such a view of the world can never change whilst the assemblage point cannot be moved, because no energy fields can be accessed other than those at that particular position, neither can those energy fields accessed be rearranged.

It is therefore obvious that perception is directly determined firstly, by the position of the assemblage point, and secondly, by the actual way in which the energy fields accessed have been arranged. This is an important point which should be grasped fully so as to avoid confusion later on.

To understand this it must be realised that the assemblage point of man is a hemisphere of intense light, roughly the size of a tennis ball. The energy fields accessed are those illuminated by this hemisphere as they pass through it. These energy fields are beams of light not much thicker than cotton threads, and therefore seers have likened them to threads of light. Being so thin, literally thousands of energy fields pass through the assemblage point to align themselves with the corresponding energy fields outside the cocoon.

However, this alignment will not necessarily be A to A, B to B, C to C, and so on, but could be A to B, or A to C, or any other possible arrangement. The energy fields outside the cocoon are identical to the ones inside, but the possible number of permutations for aligning them are truly awesome. What dictates this choice of alignment and exactly how that alignment is effected is as yet a mystery, even for the most advanced seers. Suffice it to say that this is apparently accomplished through

---

** The term used when referring to the energy of alignment in an individual being, as opposed to universal power which is denoted simply as power.*

some obscure property of *intent*.

To further clarify this concept we must define two expressions; namely, a *movement* of the assemblage point, as opposed to a *shift* of the assemblage point. Although there is a discrepancy amongst some of the Toltec lineages as to how these two expressions should be defined, this discrepancy is of such a minor consequence as to be negligible. For the purposes of this book I will give the accepted traditional definitions.

A *movement* of the assemblage point is defined as *rotating* the assemblage point within its normal position so as to bring about a different *arrangement* of the energy fields. This is much like turning the dial on a radio in order to improve upon the quality of sound received from that particular broadcasting station. A *shift* of the assemblage point is when the assemblage point is *relocated* to access a totally different group of energy fields. This shift can be to any other position on the surface of the cocoon, or into its interior.

It is the arrangement of energy fields within a specific alignment which accounts firstly, for one's own particular view of the world, and secondly, for one's ability to communicate. If we meet someone who uses the same permutation of alignment as ourself, then the arrangement would be A to A, B to B, and so on. With such a person we have a wondeful rapport and there is no difficulty in communicating. But if, on the other hand, we meet someone who uses a permutation diametrically opposed to our own the communication is terrible. With such a person we are constantly talking at cross purposes and understanding between ourself and that person becomes very much a hit-and-miss affair.

The point here is that unless we are capable of moving the assemblage point, our perception is rigidly fixed and so too is our view of the world. It is this fixation which causes repetition and ultimately habitual actions, no matter whether these are physical, emotional or mental. However, the reverse is equally true, for repetition in itself fixes the assemblage point ever more firmly, and also gives rise to monotony and boredom. Once boredom has set in our level of awareness begins to suffer dramatically, because repetitive perception soon starts to become subliminal. This is the beginning of a vicious circle in which we become progressively less aware, as our perception becomes ever more repetitive and boring.

In this respect it is interesting to note the difference between adults and children. Children have a naturally fluid assemblage point until they have been forced to fix it through social conditioning. As a result, children are able to move their assemblage points quite spontaneously. Through this movement they obviously effect constant changes within their perception, which in turn gives rise not only to novelty, but also to an abundance of vitality and enthusiasm.

In order to move the assemblage point we need *personal power.* Just like everything else we do needs energy, so too does the movement or shift of the assemblage point. In fact, even just to keep the assemblage point fixed we need to use a considerable amount of *personal power.*

Obviously, if the assemblage point is fixed and our view of the world is likewise fixed, then the amount of *personal power* we have is proportional to our level of perception, by virtue of the fact that *personal power* is the product of perception. Perception, however, is in turn proportional to the level of awareness. If, therefore, we are half asleep as a result of being 'bored out of our minds', we do not register perception very well.

The lack of registered perception does not mean that *personal power* is not being generated, but rather that all the *personal power* generated is being consumed by those habitual and repetitious acts, physical, emotional and mental, which keep the assemblage point fixed.

If then we have no surplus of *personal power* with which to move the assemblage point, where must we find this extra *power*? The solution is really quite simple, yet rather more difficult to implement than to explain.

If all our *personal power* is being consumed by our habits then obviously we must cut out all unnecessary acts. We must also dismantle our view of the world, because it is this rigid view which perpetuates habit and therefore keeps the assemblage point fixed. To begin with, the only way in which we can really do this is by being wide awake, that is, fully alert at all times. Only by being more aware of everything in our lives can we begin to differentiate between what is important, and what can rightfully be classified as unnecessary.

Warriors are ever admonished to pay special attention to all the little things in their daily lives. For it is the sum total of all these apparently insignificant details which constitutes our general behaviour, and which also reveals to us our view of the world.

In working with this it is vital to understand that by *wanting* to be fully aware, we are in fact *intending* perception. This is a crucial and indispensable prerequisite for walking the Warrior's Path. It will be remembered that in the Truths of Awareness it is stated that it is *intent* which causes us to perceive. We will not at this point venture into a definition of *intent*, but let it suffice for now to state that the more we *intend* to be aware, the greater will be our perception, and hence the more *personal power* will be generated.

THERE IS NO MAGIC – THERE IS ONLY INTENT.

WHAT FOOLS PERCEIVE AS BEING MAGIC IS BUT THE MANIPULATION OF INTENT, THEREFORE A MAGICIAN IS MERELY A MASTER OF INTENT.

The importance of *intending* to be fully aware does not end here, for there is far more to this crucial act. By struggling to perceive we are in actual fact exercising our *intent*. Because it is the force of *intent* which makes us perceive, it is of course also this same force which indirectly accounts for the placement of the assemblage point. Therefore by maintaining our view of the world we are in reality using the force of *intent* to keep the assemblage point fixed at that particular spot.

From all of this it should now be clear why it is so very important to dismantle our view of the world. To do this we must be fully aware of every little detail in our daily lives so that we can recognize that view for what it is, and what exactly it is we do in order to maintain it. Once we can clearly see our view of the world and how we maintain it, it is a relatively simple matter to dismantle that view through the technique of not-doing.

This brings us to the concept of *hunting power*. It should by now be very clear what is meant by this. To hunt *power* is to look for ways in which we can increase our level of *personal power*, so that we will achieve a fluid assemblage point.

In handling this concept it is important to bear in mind that we are all inherently lazy. It is always a lot easier to dream and talk about having *power* than actively to pursue it. Yet, if we are to have *power* we must act – we must hunt *power*, and hunt it well.

> *A HUNTER IS AN EXCEPTIONALLY DISCIPLINED MAN, FOR THE PARAMETERS OF HIS LIVELIHOOD ARE PRECISE.*

A hunter is intelligent enough not to assume that the prey he seeks will just walk over politely and accidently fall into his cooking pot. Therefore, the hunter leads a very disciplined life, meaning that the hunter is totally dedicated to hunting. The hunter is a *disciple* of hunting in the truest possible sense of the word, and therefore he directs all his efforts towards learning everything possible about hunting.

A HUNTER LIVES THE HUNT TO THE FULL; ONLY THEN CAN HE BE SUCCESSFUL.

It has already been stated that in order to hunt *power* we must be fully aware at all times. This in effect means that we must *live* awareness. The hunter who is only occasionally aware will not be a very good hunter. Before long he will doubtless fall prey to some predator stronger than him. But to be aware all the time is quite a battle for those people who have become accustomed to being half asleep. Therefore some serious changes are required within our lives before we can become hunters worthy of the name.

TRUE CHANGES ARE NEVER EASY – A MAN WILL ONLY CHANGE UNDER THOSE CIRCUMSTANCES IN WHICH HE IS FORCED TO CHANGE.

SOMETIMES EVEN IF A MAN IS FORCED TO CHANGE HE WILL STUPIDLY REFUSE UNLESS HE CAN SEE THE ADVANTAGE IN CHANGING.

Unfortunately though, whenever a man is called upon to make a change in his life one invariably hears the same old hackneyed complaints: 'I don't have a problem, but you should see my wife! I swear to you, she has problems galore! If I could only convince her of her shortcomings we would all be able to live in peace.' This type of comment is typical of average man, no matter whether he is complaining about his wife, his relatives, his boss, his job, or just life in general. It is commonly known as the *blame game*, *passing the buck*, *skirting the issue*, or to put it rather bluntly, *fart-arsing around*.

Instead of blaming everyone around him, a good hunter takes stock of his life, and brings about those changes which he deems necessary at that moment.

A GOOD HUNTER WILL CHANGE HIS WAYS WHENEVER THE NEED ARISES.

TRUE CHANGES ARE ALWAYS CATACLYSMIC IN QUALITY AND ARE EVER TRIGGERED BY WHAT APPEARS TO BE A SMALL AND INSIGNIFICANT ACT. HUNTERS WATCH FOR THESE ACTS, IN THEMSELVES AND IN THEIR PREY, AND THEREFORE ARE NOT CAUGHT OFF-GUARD BY THE EFFECTS OF THESE ACTS.

We should not be fooled into believing that we can change our lives gradually, for such changes are not really changes, but are instead ways we have devised in order to make our old habits look a little more fresh and spruced-up. Through these actions we can feel better about ourselves by pretending that we have changed our ways.

The only known change within nature which can be termed gradual is the aging process, but this aging process applies only to the physical or material form. A stubborn man does not become less stubborn with age, he only appears to be less stubborn because his body has grown weaker and therefore he has less energy to be cantankerous. If you prod such an old man even just a little you will quickly see him rise to the occasion and revert to his old habits. All true changes, even those within nature, are always abrupt and far-reaching.

THE ONLY WORTHWHILE CHANGES ARE THOSE MADE WITH SOBRIETY.

It is also important to understand that for a change to be valid it must be a sober change, that is, made consciously and wilfully. It does happen occasionally that a person will bring about changes in his life as a result of some turbulent emotional upheaval. However, most of the time such changes wear off again relatively quickly. For example, a man could change his ways as a result of severe shock, perhaps through an illness or an accident, but as time begins its healing process the shock gradually diminishes in its effect and soon the man is up to all his old tricks again.

In order to succeed upon the Path of Knowledge an all-encompassing change is required. You must transform the island of the tonal.

Man is essentially pure spirit, termed the nagal, but at birth he takes to himself a physical vehicle termed the tonal.

The tonal is the personality of man. It is like a physical island existing within the boundless ocean of pure being, the nagal. On this island is everything the incarnated individual needs for life upon the physical plane.

The *island of the tonal* encompasses every single thing which we regard as being part of ourselves, directly and indirectly. The *tonal* is the physical body, the emotional structure and the mind. Our thoughts, our feelings, our actions upon the physical plane all are part of the *tonal.* If I am poor, then it is my *tonal* which is poor, because the *nagal,* the spirit, cannot possibly be poor. Likewise if I am ill, then it is my *tonal* which is ill. If I am angry, then again it is my *tonal* which is angry. If I lack *personal power,* it is my *tonal* that is lacking. In short, the *tonal* is the luminous cocoon and all the energy fields contained within it.

Generally speaking, if we have a name for something, or are able to describe it in any way, then it is a feature of the *island of the tonal.* This is true of man as well as the universe, for the *tonal* is the state of manifestation in all of its countless differentiations, physical, emotional, mental and even that which we define as being spiritual. The *nagal,* on the other hand, is pure spirit or pure being, meaning thereby the spirit unmanifest. The *tonal* is Some-Thing, whereas the *nagal* is No-Thing.

Everything in our lives is a feature of our own particular *island of the tonal.* These features are quite literally the landscape of the island, and therefore constitute what we call our view of the world. If aggression is a feature of our island, then aggression will form part of our view of the world. Likewise, if the state of poverty is a feature of our island, then we automatically view ourselves as being poor, and whilst we maintain this view we will always lack the necessary means to make money.

Neither the island, nor the features of that island are a problem in themselves. It is not that the island is bad, or that its features are bad. It is rather the way in which the various features of the island have been landscaped that tends to create the problems in our lives and which makes the island either a paradise or a hell-hole. It is important to remember that every single thing on the island is necessary for our life upon the physical plane, and therefore not even one feature of that island can be lost or destroyed. In fact, whenever we do try to get rid of any feature we very quickly discover how impossible this is.

Therefore the task of the apprentice is to transform completely the *island of the tonal.* He must reconstruct the landscaping. By this it is meant that the apprentice must not only reconstruct the features, but he must also rearrange them so that everything is located in its correct spot on his island. By doing this the features will then co-exist in harmony with each other and with the man himself, and the apprentice will turn his island not only into a place of practical use and hospitality, but also, depending on his ability and temperament, a place of great beauty.

In order to clarify this, let us look at the example of aggression. In doing this we will be very graphic and liken aggression to a sword. Now if aggression features as part of a man's makeup he can look at his aggression and decide that it is an ugly and dangerous weapon. Fearing that people will think poorly of him for being aggressive, the man may spend years trying to get rid of his aggression, and during all this time may hide his sword as best he can. In fact, he may hide it so well that nobody will ever believe that he is aggressive. Such a man will feel that even if he has not been able to rid himself of his aggression, then at least he has it firmly under control.

This is one option, and the one which the majority of people take. However, it is a poor option for, having hidden his sword and by refusing to use it, the man never learns how to handle that sword properly. The man has suppressed his aggression and, as in all cases of suppressed emotions, a day will come when the man is pushed so tightly into a corner that he will suddenly reach for that sword. When he has it in his hands, years of suppressed aggression well up in one mighty torrent of overwhelming rage and, not knowing how to wield the sword properly, the man flails it around in uncontrolled destruction. In his inexperience in handling the sword, the man not only severely damages everybody and everything around him, but he also invariably wounds himself.

Clearly, this is not a viable option for a hunter, who has to be able to use all his weapons with skill. The apprentice to the Warrior's Path must acknowledge his aggression, not suppress it. This does not mean that the apprentice, or the hunter for that matter, has free rein to exercise that aggression on the world around him, but rather that he must learn to use it constructively and expertly should the need arise.

By acknowledging his aggression, and by carefully practising with that sword, the apprentice in time becomes a skilled swordsman, totally proficient in the handling of his sword. Aggression, which is a feature of this man's makeup, has not been lost from his *island of the tonal*, but instead has been turned into a valuable asset fully under his control. Should the need arise, such a man will reach for his sword in the twinkling of an eye, and before you even know what has hit you he will have given you a clean shave, if that is what is required. No lasting harm will have been done, because your beard will grow back, if you insist on having a beard, but you will never again mess with that man. Yet, deep in your heart, you will also be filled with admiration for this man, for such skill is beautiful and thrilling to behold.

The transformation of the *island of the tonal* by the restructuring of its features is the total change which is called for if one is to succeed in one's pursuit of *power*. It is not as difficult as it appears to be, for the only thing that is necessary is for us to take stock of our lives so that we may know what our assets are. For a hunter there are no bad aspects of himself, there are only potentials which have not been fully developed. A potential which has not yet been developed is of course a shortcoming on his island, but the hunter knows that in time it will no longer be a shortcoming. The undeveloped potential of swordsmanship is indeed a shortcoming, but this potential, when developed, is a most valuable skill.

YOUR WEAKNESSES ARE YOUR UNREALISED POTENTIALS.

If we are to succeed in hunting *power* we need all of our potential. Social conditioning may teach us that much of our potential is bad, but this is only the means by which our fellow men keep us in bondage to them and their view of the world. No hunter can ever be restrained in this way. The hunter is a free and fluid being who walks a path with a heart. For him there is no heart in an island which consists of psychic bondage, suppressed emotions and rigidity of thought.

On the hunter's island we find incredible beauty in the skill with which that island has been structured and, since he is a fluid being, the hunter is very willing to reshape his island whenever the need arises. For him such changes bring yet more exciting challenges, and who knows what undiscovered treasures of the spirit he may find in every restructuring of his *tonal*?

The secret of slipping out of the grip of social conditioning lies in the fact that the hunter places himself in a position that is beyond psychological manipulation.

> *THE HUNTER HANDLES HIS WORLD WITH SUCH CARE THAT HE LEAVES NO TRAIL BEHIND HIM. TO LEAVE A TRAIL WOULD BE TO BECOME HUNTED BY SOMETHING MORE POWERFUL THAN HIMSELF.*

This does not mean that the hunter becomes a recluse. This would be impossible, for in order to be a hunter he must operate in the world and be very much a part of it. Therefore the hunter does not try to hide from the world, but rather ensures that he does not allow himself to become the *hunted*.

> *THE ART OF THE HUNTER LIES IN HIS ABILITY TO CHOOSE BOTH THE TIMING AND THE LOCATION OF HIS APPEARANCE. BY DOING THIS HIS INTERACTION WITH THE WORLD BECOMES CALCULATED AND FRUGAL, AND THUS THE HUNTER AVOIDS DEPLETING BOTH HIMSELF AND THE WORLD AROUND HIM.*

> *THE HUNTER IS CONFIDENT IN HIS ABILITIES AS A HUNTER AND THEREFORE DOES NOT FEEL THE NEED TO WORRY.*

> *WORRY CAUSES MAN TO CLING FRANTICALLY TO HIS WORLD, WHATEVER THAT WORLD MAY BE, AND BY CLINGING HE DEPLETES BOTH HIMSELF AND HIS WORLD.*

The principal reason why people tend to become the hunted

is because they have no real confidence in themselves, and therefore they always seek approval and support from those around them. Obviously, if people behave like this, they will never escape the clutches of social conditioning, and so will remain for ever at the mercy of others. In this context we see that worry is the most debilitating cause of dependancy. People will find all sorts of things to worry about and, without even realising what it is they are doing, they constantly undermine their own strength and confidence through their worrying.

If, for example, a man is constantly worried about his health, the worry drains his energy to such an extent that eventually he does develop all manner of aches, pains and illnesses.

Likewise, if a woman is constantly in doubt about whether or not her husband truly loves her, she will, through her behaviour, cling to him so frantically that in the end he will become exhausted in trying to reassure her. Consequently, such a man will push away his wife, not because he does not love her, but simply because he will feel the need to have some space. This of course will only make the woman feel even more insecure and even more demanding of his attention. In time, the man could feel so driven from home that he might begin seeking comfort in the arms of another woman.

In these two examples one can see clearly the effects of worry, and how people manage to materialize their worst fears through worrying. Sadly though, both the man and the woman will probably never realise that they have only themselves to thank for their misfortune. Instead, they will tend to believe that the outcome was only the result of what they had always suspected to be true.

The hunter, on the other hand, trusts in his ability to hunt, and therefore has the confidence to know that he does not have to worry. But in order to have such confidence one must cultivate it by choosing how one interacts with the world around one. The hunter chooses not to seek the approval or the support of others. He does not make this choice out of any sense of arrogance or aloofness, but simply because he has enough self-respect to acknowledge his own abilities and worth. As a result of his self-respect the hunter also harbours a very deep respect for the world around him, for he knows that if he is to live off the land he must live in harmony with it.

THE HUNTER IS INTIMATELY FAMILIAR WITH HIS WORLD, YET REMAINS DETACHED FROM IT.

It is through this *detachment* that the hunter does not become affected by the world around him. However, the fact that the hunter is intimately familiar with his world means that he is detached in the sense of choosing how he will interact with his world, but not detached in the sense of not caring about it. This is a most important distinction, and something which requires considerable skill in execution.

No hunter could ever be successful if he did not know every intimate detail of his world. However, the danger in this is to become so involved with the world that one's judgement becomes impaired. For example, a hunter could become so intimate with the game he is hunting that he finds himself incapable of hunting it. On the other hand, if the hunter did not care about his world he would then plunder it just because for him hunting was fun. In both cases the hunter will end up starving, for either he loves animals too much to hunt them, or else he depletes the stocks indiscriminately.

THE HUNTER DOES NOT PLUNDER HIS WORLD – HE TAKES FROM IT ONLY WHAT HE TRULY NEEDS. IN THIS WAY THE HUNTER ENSURES THAT HIS COFFER, WHETHER IT HOLDS FRIENDS, FOOD, HAPPINESS OR POWER, IS NEVER EMPTY.

It is important to understand that to be a hunter implies considerably more than merely to hunt. The true hunter is also something of a psychologist. Through experience he has seen the routine acts and the predictable behaviour of both man and animal, and has therefore come to know the importance of having to study the game he is hunting.

IN ORDER TO TRAP GAME THE HUNTER MUST NOT ONLY KNOW THE ROUTINES OF THAT GAME, BUT HE MUST ALSO BE ABLE TO OUTWIT HIS PREY.

If the hunter were to set his traps in such a way as to reveal his motives, the animal he hunts would not be so foolish as to walk into them. The hunter must therefore set his traps so cleverly that his prey will be unaware of them until they are sprung. The hunter is also well aware that, just as he is a predator, so there are those predators who would likewise not hestitate to hunt him, given the opportunity. So to avoid becoming prey himself, the hunter takes care not to make the same mistakes as the prey he has learned to stalk. Accordingly, the hunter sees to it that his movements and his actions are always unpredictable.

TO BE PREDICTABLE IS TO BECOME THE HUNTED.

Generally speaking, average man is so very predictable. Fixed as he is, by heavy and all-consuming routines, average man makes easy prey for anyone wishing to hunt him.

Take, for example, a man who always has his lunch at 13:00 hours at that quiet little restaurant just around the corner from his office. The man always finishes work at exactly 17:00 hours, at which time he rushes off to the station to catch the 17:25 train home. The man follows this routine five days a week, month in and month out. Anyone wishing to corner this man will have no trouble at all in doing so; all that is required is to wait for him at his favourite table in the restaurant at the allotted hour, or else at the station just before 17:25.

On the other hand, it would not be quite so simple to corner a man who only sometimes eats lunch, and when he does it is always in a different restaurant. It would also not be an easy matter to find him on his way home if he sometimes rushes home on the first train, sometimes lingers longer in the office, or sometimes first does some shopping before taking a bus to visit a friend on his way home. Clearly, such a man is unpredictable, and even though his hours at the office may be fixed, he will always find ways in which to make those hours seem unpredictable.

In these examples we have looked only at the physical routines which people follow, but it is vital to realise that habitual emotional responses and fixed thought patterns also make us vulnerable. Furthermore, to become vulnerable does not mean vulnerable only in the sense of being stalked by others, but to become exposed to the forces operating in our lives.

Whenever we become predictable we cease to be fluid. This not only makes us vulnerable, but it also fixes the assemblage point firmly in that particular view of the world prevalent at that moment. As we have already noted, it is not man's destiny to be confined to only one view of the world; man is meant to learn by experiencing all of the great many possibilities inherent within life. If, therefore, we become stuck in our view of the world, the forces of our destiny begin to stalk us in an attempt to make us fluid once more.

THE GOOD HUNTER ACKNOWLEDGES THAT THERE ARE SUPERIOR FORCES WITHIN THIS UNIVERSE WHICH GUIDE HIM AS WELL AS ALL OTHER CREATURES. THESE FORCES DICTATE THE CIRCUMSTANCES OF BOTH LIFE AND DEATH.

This most important point not only serves as a reminder that we are stalked by both predator and the forces of destiny, but it also directly addresses the question of ethics and morality. Apart from material wealth, the concepts of ethics and morality frequently plague and confuse man and cause him more worry than anything else. In fact, questions surrounding money, ethics and morality generally keep man firmly entrenched in his social conditioning.

When a hunter needs to eat he sets his trap, and if upon his return he finds an animal in that trap he slaughters it immediately in quiet gratitude. The hunter knows that it was neither his cleverness nor his trap which ensnared the animal, but rather the forces of destiny which guided that animal into his trap.

That particular animal's destiny was to feed that hunter. Knowing this, the hunter does not take pity upon the animal and set it free, for to do so would be to deny that animal its destiny. No hunter who is worthy of the name will ever aspire to interfere in the destiny of another being. Such an act would be to imply that he is wiser than those forces which dictate the lives and the deaths of all creatures, including himself. No true hunter would ever assume such arrogance.

> *IN THE FINAL ANALYSIS WHAT ELSE IS MORE IMPORTANT THAN LIFE AND DEATH? THE FORCES WHICH COMMAND THESE TRULY RULE ALL CREATURES.*

Pity is one of the worst crimes against humanity; in fact, against all life-forms in general. We should always beware of those do-gooders who take pity upon everyone and everything around them. Such people have no respect for another being's destiny, and their only aim in life is to meddle and interfere where they are not needed. These people will always protest very loudly under the banner of morality and common decency, but they never stop to consider the possible effects of their actions. Individuality, and the full development of awareness, always suffer at the hands of these people, no matter what they claim their motives to be.

There are times when help is genuinely called for and at such times a hunter gives his assistance willingly and unreservedly; but a hunter will never give help if he can see that such help is not called for. To render assistance when it is not needed is to do the other person an injustice.

The hunter does not presume to interfere with the forces which guide the lives and deaths of all creatures, but by the same token he takes full responsibility for his actions. If he finds two animals in his trap when he only needs one, he will take only one animal and set the other free. Taking both animals would mean that the hunter has succumbed either to greed or to worry, and this of course would render him vulnerable. Furthermore, the hunter treats his world with infinite care, and as a result does not plunder it. Such is the discipline of the hunter, and such is the impeccability of his spirit.

This discipline and impeccability is crucial in understanding the intricacies entailed in hunting *power*. Up to this point we have looked only at the training of the hunter, but obviously the purpose of this training is that he may learn to hunt the ultimate of game, namely *power*. This training is not easy, and it takes time and meticulous attention to detail in order to acquire that discipline and impeccability which a hunter needs.

Without this careful training no man will succeed in hunting *power*, because to hunt *power* is infinitely more difficult than to stalk animals or people. Not only are animals and people extremely predictable, but they are also tangible. *Power*, on the other hand, is always thoroughly unpredictable and certainly not tangible. To hunt a prey which is both intangible and unpredictable is not only the most difficult challenge in the world, but is also highly dangerous.

To stalk *power* needs infinite care and a very keen sense of awareness. The hunter who crashes through the bush like a bulldozer will not only frighten off his prey, but will also very likely fall prey to someone or something stronger than himself. In this respect it is amusing to see how many well-meaning, but nevertheless misguided, people rush off to pursue knowledge at every opportunity. These people cavort around in a kind of spiritual frenzy, loudly acclaiming all of their findings in childlike excitement. Observing them, one can only come to the conclusion that they are indeed like children – children with toy rifles, playing at being hunters.

Through his training the hunter has come to understand what it means to hunt *power*. Having gained this knowledge he does not abandon himself to the hunt, because the hunter knows that his prey, being intangible and unpredictable, could well lead him into a fatal trap. This is an important point which needs to be fully understood.

The only reason for hunting *power* is to enable us to have sufficient *personal power* to claim our freedom. But in order to claim that freedom we must also be able to claim our *personal power*, for the Eagle does not impart the gift of freedom to those who are not strong enough to fight for their *personal power*. The only way in which to become strong is to fight, and the more difficult the battle the stronger we become. It is for this reason that the hunter, unlike the average man, does not complain about the challenges in his life. The hunter knows that the greater the challenge, the greater will be his gift of *power*.

With regard to this, the hunter also knows full well that the forces which guide his life upon earth will show him no pity and grant him no mercy. For the hunter to be granted mercy would be to deny him the opportunity to fight for victory and condemn him instead to a life of slavery.

> *IF YOU ARE NOT STRONG ENOUGH TO FIGHT YOU HAVE NO CHOICE BUT TO ACCEPT THE LIFE OF A SLAVE. THE HUNTER IS A FREE BEING WHO CANNOT SUBMIT HIMSELF TO SLAVERY. FOR HIM THERE IS NO CHOICE BUT TO FIGHT. IF HE DIES IN THAT FIGHT, AT LEAST HE WILL DIE AS A FREE BEING, AND NOT AS A SLAVE.*

There comes a moment in the life of every man when he simply knows that he cannot continue being a slave. From that moment on, whether he has been trained as a hunter or not, he enters into the mood of a hunter.

No longer abandoning himself to anything, least of all slavery, the hunter does not care to throw his *personal power* away by making a foolish move. Instead, he sits down quietly to take stock of his life, and of his situation. He knows that it is he himself who has made the *bid for power*, and that it was in order to equip himself for this hunt that he has trained. The hunter also takes careful note of the rules of that hunt. The rules are simple enough, but also deadly – *give no quarter, and be granted no quarter; the winner takes all.*

In a battle in which the stakes are so high, the hunter would be a fool if he did not weigh up his options with care. If the hunter wins the battle he will have won enough *personal power* with which to claim his freedom, but if he should lose he loses everything. Clearly, the hunter cannot enter into such a battle recklessly.

> *THE HUNTER CONFORMS TO NO-ONE'S WISHES OTHER THAN HIS OWN. IF HE ENTERS INTO A COURSE OF ACTION IT IS BECAUSE HE IS FULLY AWARE OF THE POSSIBLE OUTCOME OF THOSE ACTIONS.*

> *THE HUNTER NEVER LAYS HIMSELF OPEN TO BEING VICTIMIZED. IN HIS ACTIONS HE MAKES ALLOWANCE FOR THE UNEXPECTED AND IS THEREFORE NEVER TAKEN BY SURPRISE. IN THIS WAY HE AVOIDS MOST OF WHAT FOOLS REGARD AS ACCIDENTS.*

Having taken stock of his life, the hunter realises that even though the risks are high he still has no choice other than to fight. Such is the irony of walking the Path of Knowledge. In our fight to free ourselves from the bondage of social conditioning we find ourselves having become the slaves of *power* instead.

Average man believes that he has free choice, but the hunter is a man who has come to see the futility of this belief. For him there are only two options; either he fights for his freedom from social conditioning, or he refuses to fight and joins his fellow men in their folly. Obviously, the second option is not one a hunter can accept, which in effect means that he does not have a choice.

In order to understand this fully we must remember that the hunter becomes a hunter in order to escape the confines of social conditioning. He does this so that he will have the *personal power* with which to choose his own frame of reference. Having come this far there is for the hunter no longer any possibility of turning back, because the world he has left behind is not the world he wanted any more. In the light of this he realises that he does not actually have anything to lose other than his life – but what is this life worth to him if it is spent in bondage to his fellow man?

This point in the life of a hunter is always a most poignant one. It is at this juncture that the hunter knows that he does not have a choice. However, to venture into the unknown still demands of him all his courage, and more, because he also knows that it is going to be a journey of no return. Such a journey requires that the hunter says farewell to everything he has known until then. Admittedly, the world he has known is not the world in which he wishes to remain, but it has been the only world the hunter has ever known, and even though it is filled with much that he dislikes it also holds a great many treasures of his spirit. It was after all in this world that he first learned to dream of freedom and *power*, and it was here that he took his first tentative steps in learning to become a hunter.

It is only when the hunter has reached this cross-road in his life that he truly begins to sense the impact of the forces which have guided him throughout his life. Now, in retrospect, he can see the purpose of everything that has happened to him and how those experiences have brought him to where he stands. Although his destiny is yet vague and locked into the future, he can still grasp enough to realise that his bid for *power,* and consequent training as a hunter, was all foreordained. It is then that he knows beyond any further doubt that his bid for *power* is irrevocable.

An analogy might serve to make the concept of a bid for *power* a little more comprehensible. Let us therefore consider a child, and the fact that it is apparently man's destiny to walk upright.

When a baby is born it does not walk straight away. For a long time it is perfectly content just to lie around and move its limbs at random. Then it begins to agitate to sit up, but at first can only do so when propped up with pillows. Again some time passes until the infant has gained enough muscular strength to start crawling. This is analogous to the training of the hunter. With this new-found freedom the child begins to explore its world. It is in having learned to crawl that the child now begins to distinguish between certain aspects of the world around him. Through trial and error he soon learns to take care in where he crawls, and in what he touches.

Then comes the day when the child is strong enough, and he suddenly stands up. It appears to be a simple enough act, but the change is drastic. By that act the child has made his bid to walk. The child may still lack sufficient muscular co-ordination, he may still be very wobbly in the knees and off balance, but one thing will lead to another until finally he walks, and then runs. The child's bid to walk is irreversible, because, unless he was born a cripple, it is his destiny to walk upright.

None of us can avoid the forces which guide us throughout life. Our destinies, whatever they may be, must be fulfilled. The hunter acknowledges this, and in doing so takes stock of himself and his new life. Just as the child is very unsteady in his first few tentative steps, so too is the hunter in taking his first steps upon the Path of Power.

IN STARTING OUT TO HUNT FOR POWER, THE HUNTER

KNOWS THAT HIS INEXPERIENCE WILL CAUSE HIM TO BE OFF BALANCE. BUT BY BEING WIDE AWAKE, AND BY CULTIVATING A QUIETNESS OF LIFE, HE FINDS THE NECESSARY EQUILIBRIUM OF HIS SPIRIT.

If we revert to our analogy of the child learning to walk, we see that when the child has to descend a staircase unaided for the first time he is in grave danger of hurting himself badly, perhaps even of killing himself. Yet there does not need to be any danger as long as the child approaches the staircase in full awareness, and does not try to rush down the stairs three at a time.

The hunter, remembering his training, approaches the Path of Power in just the same manner. Fully aware of the danger he faces in hunting an intangible and unpredictable prey, the hunter moves quietly and acts with great caution. In this way he begins to build the confidence he needs in order to feel stable and to fight whatever battles *power* may suddenly spring on him.

OUR IMBALANCE IS DUE TO THE SUM TOTAL OF ALL OUR ACTIONS.

This aphorism is vital to everything Toltecs understand and practise. When we run from our experiences, or ignore them, or handle them carelessly, we become off balance. However, whenever we find ourselves off balance the most natural reaction is to pause, or to stand still for a moment, in order to regain our balance. It is this *pausing* which is defined as the *quietness of life.*

Life is indisputably a continuum, but a continuum which consists of intermittent bursts of energy or pulsations. The hunter moves with the pulsations of life by pausing before every act. In this way he can focus his full attention before he leaps. By giving each act his undivided attention the hunter's judgement is impeccable and his spirit is never off balance – the hunter is *wide awake.*

Through living like this the hunter is in full control of every situation in his life. Note that I said situation. The hunter is not in control of his life as such, because this control is not in his hands but in the hands of those forces which guide his life.

Through being in control of every situation in his life the hunter has the stability and confidence necessary to enter his battle for *power.* Nevertheless he is still painfully aware of the poverty of his human resources. So the hunter experiences *fear.* Not a debilitating fear, but a fear which keeps him on his toes and wide awake. It is the fear which comes from knowing that the rules of the hunt allow for no pity and no mercy.

Knowing the rules of the hunt, and why they have to be so uncompromising, the hunter becomes filled with a deep *respect* for his opponent. In the depths of his heart the hunter senses that this battle will be a most noble one. He has no doubt that it will be rife with trickery, but he also knows that the outcome will be fair, in that the winner takes all. Such a battle, in which all is fair play and the spoils of which have been silently agreed upon with honour, is the noblest of all possible battles.

Having got this far the hunter has no other recourse than to sit quietly and to wait. He is in no hurry, for he knows that now that he has made his bid for *power* the forces which guide his destiny will seek him out and the battle will be engaged. The hunter knows that to turn coward and try to hide, or to run from the battle once it is engaged, will be of no avail for the forces of his destiny will still hunt him down and confront him around every corner. Realising that his only chance of survival is to stand his ground and fight, the hunter becomes filled with a sense of *absolute assurance.* After all, what can he lose except a life which has for him already lost all meaning?

This is how the hunter approaches his battle for *power:* he is *wide awake, fearful, respectful* and *fully assured.* This is his *shield.* In the face of the impossible odds he will be facing it is perhaps not very much, but it is all he has, and it is for this reason that he has trained long and hard to use it impeccably.

This is the nature of a hunter's fate, but his mood is not one of melancholy or pessimism. Nor does the hunter feel any cause for regret or, for that matter, resentment or bitterness. On the contrary, he feels privileged and optimistic. Privileged, because he wonders why he of all people should be so lucky as to have been singled out by *power* for combat; optimistic, because he now knows that the worst that can possibly happen to him is that his destiny will unfold, and this, after all, is what he has been seeking all along.

For the hunter this is a time of breathtaking wonder, a marvellous dream come true – a challenge which demands of him only his impeccable best, and his bravest fight. Nothing less could possibly justify the honour of such a gift.

In that moment the hunter has taken his first step upon the path of no return, because even if his bid for *power* had been reversible, he will no longer even consider turning back. We see a faint reflection of this in soldiers who have fought a war for a long time. When the war is finally over and these soldiers return home they often cannot settle down to their former lives – not even to their homes, wives or family. This is invariably rationalized in the form of some logical diagnosis, but the truth is that these men have lived for too long with the very fabric of life and death. Through their experiences they have discovered aspects of themselves, aspects of life, which have alienated them for ever from the humdrum existence they led before being drafted into the war.

> *TO SEEK OUT THE DISCIPLINED AND SKILLED WAYS OF THE HUNTER IS THE ONLY TRUE HONOUR WE MAY RIGHTFULLY CLAIM, AND TO SEEK THE IMPECCABILITY OF THE HUNTER'S SPIRIT IS THE ONLY POSSIBLE JUSTIFICATION FOR OUR EXISTENCE.*

LION

Having witnessed the very essence of life and death, there is nothing in this world a warrior cannot contend with.
(Pencil drawing: Susan Emily)

CHAPTER FIVE

THE WARRIOR'S CHALLENGE

No man can survive the Path of Knowledge if he is not prepared to embrace death. Death is a warrior's best advisor.

Having made his bid for *power*, and having been trained in the skill of hunting *power*, the hunter now only needs to gain the necessary practical experience. It is through this experience that he will graduate to the level of a *warrior*, for the only difference between a *hunter* and a *warrior* is in the degree of experience. Through his lack of experience the hunter knows very little about the practicalities involved in hunting *power*. The warrior, on the other hand, is a man who is well seasoned in the battle for *power*.

It is not up to us to decide whether or not we will become warriors; this decision lies with those forces which guide the lives of all creatures.

This aphorism often causes an apprentice undue worry and concern. If, however, it is remembered that the training of both the hunter and the warrior is identical, as is their goal, then there will be no need for concern. In the final analysis it is only the degree of practical experience gained which will make the difference between one individual and the next.

With regard to this we should always keep in mind that

experience cannot be prearranged, since it is not within the control of any person. No man can avoid or change his destiny, and it is this destiny which determines the experiences he will have in any one particular lifetime. All that is required of us is to aid in the unfoldment of our destiny by co-operating intelligently with those forces which guide us throughout our lives. By doing this we use all our opportunities and thus gain the most from our experience. It is this intelligent co-operation with the forces of our destiny which is the primary goal of the Toltec teachings. Everything the apprentice is taught, including the movement of the assemblage point, is geared towards helping him achieve this skill.

An important point which needs to be emphasised here because it is so often overlooked, is that the life experiences of the average man, of the hunter and of the warrior, form a triangle which is vital to the total being of the true Toltec. When this triangle is overlooked people tend to labour under the erroneous idea that to be a Toltec means somehow to foresake the world. This could not be further from the truth, for a warrior, like the hunter, never forsakes the world, since to do so would be to foresake his humanness.

These three types of life experience are three distinct, but nevertheless interactive and therefore interdependent *qualities* of human awareness. These three qualities of awareness must be refined to their maximum potential by every apprentice and applied most carefully in his life. It is insanity to suppose that any man can become a *man of knowledge* by denying himself those very qualities which constitute his humanness. Everything upon the *island of the tonal* is there for the simple reason that we need it in order to gain the necessary experience to become warriors. Not a single thing upon that island can or may be lost, and this includes our different levels or qualities of awareness.

Both the hunter and the warrior understand that the only true purpose of human existence upon earth is to achieve *total awareness.* Through his experience the warrior has also come to the realisation that knowledge is in reality *power*.

This is not so difficult to grasp if we remember that *power* is the energy of alignment. When we gain knowledge through experience, it means that we have perceived something through that experience of which we were not aware before. Such perception is of course the result of an alignment which, in turn, has generated *power*. Needless to say, this applies only to *knowledge*, and not to *information*. We should always remember that information is mere theory, whilst knowledge is something gained from experience. Unless they are put into practice, information and theory have ***no*** *power*, but knowledge ***is*** *power*.

Therefore if we are to have *power* we must make the best possible use of all our experiences. This in effect means that we must strive to *perceive* as much as possible. It is this striving for perception which constitutes the hunt for *power*, but since *power* is an intangible and unpredictable opponent, life for the warrior becomes an endless challenge.

> *THE WARRIOR LIVES BY CHALLENGE; THEREFORE HIS LIFE IS A DISCIPLINED STRATEGY.*

Obviously one cannot be successful in hunting *power* if one is living an undisciplined life in a semiconscious state. To hunt *power*, as we have already seen, demands of us the disciplined ways and constant vigilance of the hunter. This requirement of discipline, though, can often be misconstrued. In his efforts to be fully alert the apprentice will desperately try to analyse and understand every occurrence in his daily life. There is nothing wrong with this provided that the apprentice does not forget that all the information he gathers in this way will necessarily be subject to his view of the world.

To seek the meaning of our experiences is good and proper, because only in this way can we arrive at knowledge, but to make the mistake of assuming that those meanings are the only possible reality is to court disaster. It is of paramount importance to remember that all meanings change as the assemblage point is made to move or shift. Therefore, any meaning which is attached to an experience is only a fraction of the truth, and at the end of the day fractional truth is not the whole truth. If we were to hunt a lion, and managed only to get a small piece of its mane, then we must acknowledge the fact that the lion itself escaped us.

> *A WARRIOR DOES NOT CARE ABOUT MEANINGS. IN DEALING WITH AN OPPONENT WHICH IS INTANGIBLE AND UNPREDICTABLE MEANING LOSES ITS SIGNIFICANCE. IN VIEW OF THIS, RATIONALIZATIONS ARE A DANGEROUS WASTE OF TIME AND ENERGY.*

To become excited about having arrived at a meaning for an experience is tantamount to becoming excited about having acquired a small piece of the lion's mane. The truth is that the lion has eluded us, and we have acquired only a fragment of knowledge. The fragment of knowledge gained is good, but only in so far as it aids us to become stronger and wiser in the continuing hunt for *power*.

This, more often than not, is the precise point where an apprentice will walk blindly into the trap of rationalization. Forgetting that he has acquired only a fraction of the knowledge available from his experience, he happily begins to theorise upon his newly acquired knowledge. Before long, the hunt for *power* has been forgotten and the rush for intellectualism is on.

This is not to imply that a warrior does not stop to think and to weigh up his options. On the contrary, a warrior takes infinite care in noting the minutest detail in his life, and he considers every situation meticulously. He does this, not because he feels the need to find meaning in the situation, but because he needs *clarity* in order to act efficiently.

> *THERE EXISTS A VERY FINE LINE BETWEEN MEANING AND CLARITY. THE WARRIOR SEEKS CLARITY IN ANY SITUATION, RATHER THAN ITS MEANING.*

Any situation which arises in our lives is a challenge, in that it gives us the opportunity to learn. In accepting this challenge we automatically attach some kind of meaning to the situation. But since that meaning will be based upon our present frame of reference it will obviously also be limited, and it is vital that we remember this. The warrior, being well aware of this, does not waste unnecessary time and energy in rationalising about such meanings. Instead he uses the meaning he has gained in order to achieve that clarity of vision which will reveal to him his next step in pursuing the situation at hand.

The difference between meaning and clarity is not always easy to see, but an example will help make this clearer. Consider a situation in which a man accuses his wife of overspending.

If the woman becomes obsessed with trying to work out what her husband means by accusing her of wasting money, she will spend a great deal of time and energy in an attempt to justify her spending. Such justifications will lead to endless arguments about who is right and how best money should be utilised. Even worse, though, is the likelihood that through their arguing, both the man and his wife will become embroiled in useless attacks upon each other's characters. In the heat of the argument they will defend themselves and their viewpoints with desperate conviction. In the end, each feeling equally attacked by the other, they will even start making assertions about which neither of them are certain.

This is the kind of trap about which the warrior is extremely cautious. If the woman had been a warrior she would not have allowed herself to get caught up in meanings, but would instead have concentrated on seeing the situation as an opportunity to gain knowledge. She would have done this, firstly by acknowledging the challenge posed by the accusation, and secondly, by striving for the necessary clarity in the situation.

Having acknowledged the face value of her husband's words, the woman will turn her attention to whether or not she does indeed lack experience in handling money. In order to be honest with herself the woman cannot afford to get caught up in trying to justify her spending. Instead she must realise the need to examine her husband's complaints, and then to take very careful note of how she does use money. Only in this way can she achieve the necessary clarity that will enable her to gain knowledge.

If, after due consideration, the woman comes to the conclusion that she can learn something useful from her husband about using money, she would be a fool to refuse his advice and help. If on the other hand, she can clearly see that her use of money is faultless, then the woman will have to review the entire situation. Should the woman now feel that her husband's accusations are false, she will be fully entitled to ignore his complaints. However, this alone will not be the answer, simply because we cannot avoid our problems by disregarding them.

WARRIORS WIN BATTLES, NOT BY IGNORING THEM, BUT THROUGH CLARITY.

As a warrior, the woman now realises that her spending is not the real issue and that the accusation is obviously aimed at something else. In other words, the true challenge lies elsewhere.

In this example it is clear to see that the warrior is required to have a great deal of honesty and sobriety. It is never easy to accept a situation objectively when our integrity is being challenged. It is a very human reaction immediately to start defending ourselves by trying to justify our actions. Yet such a reaction always leads us into the trap of strengthening our view of the world, and thus we keep ourselves firmly entrenched in the conditions from which we are trying to escape.

ONLY A WARRIOR CAN SURVIVE THE BATTLE FOR POWER.

The only way of avoiding the traps of our own human condition is to live like a warrior, and in doing so to regard every situation in our lives as a challenge in the hunt for *power*.

> *HAVING TRAINED AS A HUNTER, THE WARRIOR HANDLES EACH OF HIS CHALLENGES WITH THE UTMOST RESPECT.*

By cultivating this attitude towards the situations which arise within his life, the warrior gains a great deal of respect for everything he encounters. Therefore, even if someone insults him, the warrior does not lose his control, because he sees that insult for the challenge it is. It is not that the warrior has respect for the insult itself, but rather that he respects the *opportunity* the challenge brings him. In this way the warrior achieves not only clarity, but also that *control* which is so vital in dealing with an opponent that is intangible and unpredictable. In acting like this the warrior can never fall into the trap of taking anything at its face value.

The importance in all of this is to realise that man constantly feels compelled to seek explanations which will put his mind at rest, for the unknown is not only frightening, but also produces a sense of insecurity and unease.

> *THE ERROR OF MAN IS TO SEEK EXPLANATIONS WHICH SUBSTANTIATE HIS VIEW OF THE WORLD. THE UNKNOWN CANNOT BE EXPLAINED IN THIS WAY. AS A RESULT, ALL EXPLANATIONS TURN INTO A MATTER OF BLIND FAITH OR SUPERSTITION.*

There is nothing wrong in seeking suitable explanations, except that it never occurs to man that in doing so he is merely shaping the world around him into what he would like to believe it to be. Man is forever trying to explain everything in the world with *desired explanations*, which may placate his reasoning mind, but often have very little to do with the truth. In this way man constantly maintains his view of the world, and thus also keeps his assemblage point firmly fixed.

Provided that his explanations more or less fit his view of the world, man is happy and feels secure. However, so strong is his belief in his own explanations that when something happens to challenge them the man becomes confused and uncertain. Suddenly he finds his view of the world rocked, and he is forced either to re-evaluate his explanations or, unfortunately and more often than not, to start defending those explanations in an attempt to justify and secure them.

EXPLANATIONS ARE NOT REALITY – ONLY A MAKESHIFT ARRANGEMENT OF THE WORLD.

There is no need for any man to claim confusion if he realises that all explanations are merely products of a temporary view of the world. An analogy will help make this clear. Let us consider that during a walk in the mountains you find a plant you have never seen before, that you study it carefully and come to some conclusions about it. Perhaps you feel that the plant is something akin to a wild rose. Content that you have been able to identify this plant in some way you happily continue on your walk.

Some time after this you happen to walk into an exhibition of wild plants. There you discover that what you thought was a wild rose is in fact a bramble bush, which does not even belong to the rose family. If at that moment, you acknowledge that your assumption had merely been a calculated guess, you would feel no confusion. If, on the other hand, you feel convinced that the plant you saw in the mountains was a wild rose, you would be utterly confused by the information which now confronts you.

Similarly, if we choose to remember that our view of the world is only a makeshift interpretation of the unknown, we can never be confused or surprised when that view is challenged.

However, if we believe that our view is indisputable, then we leave no room for other possibilities, and sooner or later confusion must reign supreme.

CONFUSION IS A WILFULLY INDUCED STATE OF MIND. WE CAN ENTER OR EXIT IT AT WILL.

MAN DELIBERATELY CONFUSES HIMSELF IN ORDER TO PLEAD IGNORANCE.

Confusion is a most convenient escapism used by man whenever he has to face something that frightens him, or that he does not like. However, we are always fully aware of what we are doing, even though we may choose not to acknowledge our true motives.

MAN'S REASON PURPOSEFULLY PARADES AS THE INFALLIBLE JUDGE IT FANCIES ITSELF TO BE. UNFORTUNATELY THOUGH, LIFE IS INFINITELY BIGGER THAN MAN'S REASON.

Our reason is mostly far too big for its boots and imagines itself capable of a job for which it was never intended. Reason's only purpose is to enable us to discriminate wisely, and to do computations. Instead reason tries to assume the role of understanding, but it never occurs to our reason that within a fluid universe there is very little to understand.

IN AN UNKNOWN UNIVERSE PERVADED BY THE UNPREDICTABLE QUIRKS OF POWER, UNDERSTANDING IS OF VERY LITTLE SIGNIFICANCE.

Understanding is merely a justification for unnecessary rationalizations. Take as an example a duckling which has to swim for the first time. The duckling does not first have to understand the laws of flotation before it can swim – it simply walks into the water, and instinctively swims.

Likewise, when a child is learning to walk, we don't first instruct him on the laws of gravity and muscular co-ordination. Instead we do something quite irrational; we simply encourage the child to perform what is in fact a miracle. The child will walk long before he understands anything about the complex laws concerning gravity and anatomy. Yet man's reason chooses to ignore facts such as these.

Reason will always persist in trying to find logical explanations for everything encountered, even if this means having to force a square peg into a round hole. However, if reason is incapable of arriving at a suitable understanding of an event, it will often resort to the irrational act of totally denying what has taken place.

THE WARRIOR, KNOWING THAT THERE IS NOTHING TO UNDERSTAND, ACKNOWLEDGES A BARRIER WHEN HE COMES TO IT, AND THEN JUMPS OVER IT.

When the warrior encounters a problem in his life he puts his mind at rest by acknowledging it for the obstacle it is, but instead of getting caught up in rationalizations in an effort to understand the problem, he simply tackles it immediately. Problems in themselves have no value other than to make us emotionally stronger, mentally more agile and spiritually wiser.

Soldiers, like athletes, are often made to traverse obstacle courses as part of their training. They know that the purpose of every obstacle is to force them into bringing out from within themselves potentials which would otherwise not have surfaced. The problems a warrior has to face in life serve the same purpose. The only understanding of any importance to the warrior is the understanding of himself and of his potential, and it is to this end that all his problems lead him.

It is not just the situations which arise in our lives that provide us with obstacles, but also our so-called *dark side*, or *vices*. Here it is important to realise once again the crippling restraints of social conditioning. From early childhood men and woman are taught to hide those aspects of themselves that are deemed unworthy of human behaviour. Yet it should always be remembered that no person can be whole if he denies aspects of himself.

DENIAL IS THE WORST FORM OF SELF-INDULGENCE.

A WARRIOR SEES HIS FAULTS AS BEING HIS PASSAGE TO POWER.

Generally speaking, man is forever caught up in trying to justify his behaviour, and in seeking rational explanations for everything in his life. It is disconcerting how often one hears statements like: 'If I had only known what I know today I would have chosen a different career. If only I had done a degree I would not today be struggling to make a living. If only I did not have so many problems in my life I would be able to spend more time in trying to live like a warrior.' Such reasoning is absurd, and yet people indulge in it constantly, forgetting that everything in our lives is just perfect the way it is, and that every obstacle is there to equip us to handle *power*.

NO MAN CAN CLAIM THAT HE WOULD HAVE POWER IF HIS LIFE OR CIRCUMSTANCES WERE DIFFERENT.

It is the bane of our human condition to believe that the problems in our lives stop us from realising our full potential. All our problems are challenges, gifts of *power*, which present us with the most marvellous opportunity to fight our way to freedom. This we have already seen in the previous chapter.

It is especially important to acknowledge our dark sides as well as our so-called failings or faults. Admittedly, this is not an easy task. As a result of our social conditioning we normally suffer severe feelings of guilt and failure whenever we are brought face to face with our faults. Yet we should always remember that our faults are simply our unrealised potentials – potentials which have not yet been brought into the light of full control.

What precludes most people from achieving their freedom is the fact that they feel guilty about standing up for their rights and claiming what is rightfully theirs. A warrior has no compunction in claiming what is his, regardless of whether it is money, respect, love, knowledge, or his dark side.

Through looking at our faults carefully we come to the realisation that each one has a virtue hidden within it. Therefore, our faults must be studied meticulously and then transmuted into the potentials they are. Only then can we be truly whole and free. The dark side of man is dark indeed, and this no warrior will deny; but to hide that darkness, pretending it is not there, is gross stupidity.

People usually refuse to look at their dark sides because they fear to acknowledge their shortcomings, even to themselves. Such fear is based upon the fact that man worries continually about having to maintain his self-image amongst his fellow men. It is ironic, though, that whenever a man is faced with certain death, he spontaneously acts only for survival. In such moments, the man does not even pause to consider his image; unselfishness can suddenly turn into gross selfishness, and bravery into sheer cowardice.

THE WARRIOR COMES TO KNOWLEDGE FULLY PREPARED TO DIE, AND THUS CIRCUMVENTS ALL POSSIBLE PITFALLS.

BEING PREPARED FOR THE WORST, THE WARRIOR CANNOT BE SURPRISED, BECAUSE HE IS NOT EXPECTING TO LIVE.

FACING DEATH, THE WARRIOR CUTS OUT ALL UNNECESSARY ACTS; THEREFORE HIS FATE UNFOLDS SMOOTHLY.

So many of the debilitating effects of social conditioning can be eradicated if we ackowledge the fact that death is constantly stalking us. Man has somehow managed to convince himself that he is guaranteed a long life. Believing this, he naturallly has all the time in the world to indulge in all sorts of fears, doubts and pettiness. However, in the face of death, nearly all such fears and pettiness dwindle away into total insignificance. The warrior knows this, just as he knows that the concept of immortality is a fool's idea. No-one can possibly justify the belief that he is going to live beyond the present hour.

Realising this, the warrior embraces his death. By keeping in mind that he could die at any moment, the warrior cuts out everything that hampers him in seeking his freedom. Not expecting to live, the warrior very neatly circumvents the traps of social conditioning, because he is not plagued by the foolishness of having to worry about his self-image.

Moreover, through adopting this stance, the warrior does not have to concern himself with the outcome of his actions. This is not to imply that the warrior acts recklessly. On the contrary, because the warrior is hunting *power*, he acts with infinite care, but, unlike average man, he is not concerned with having to win. Victory can only have significance if one is going to survive the battle.

One of the worst pitfalls of believing in longevity is man's endless string of expectations. Whenever we expect something we lay ourselves wide open to surprise, disappointment, and generally speaking, disaster. In order to grasp this more fully, consider a soldier who has to flee for his life.

The only way open to the soldier is to flee through a terrain which he knows to be riddled with landmines. Time is running out fast, and therefore the soldier does not have the time to indulge in petty doubts or fears. If he stays where he is, the enemy will cut him down, but if he flees into the fatal terrain he may have a very slim chance of surviving.

Such a soldier is wide awake and alert. He is not disappointed in finding himself faced with this challenge. He is quick to realise that his enemies, having planted the landmines themselves, are not likely to follow him. Not expecting to live, the soldier sees this route, deadly as it is, as his only hope of survival.

To be taken by surprise in a terrain such as this would be lethal, therefore the soldier moves with utmost caution. The only thing called for in a situation such as this is keen awareness and precise judgement. The soldier knows that a foot placed hurriedly or carelessly will spell instant annihilation. Life, for this soldier, is now being measured step by step, second by second.

In this tension, the soldier finds within himself potentials he never knew he possessed. His senses have become more acute than they have ever been, and he experiences an inner silence in which there is no temptation to think about anything else other than where next to place his feet. Time seems to have stopped, for so intense is the soldier's concentration that he does not dare think about how far he has travelled, or about how much further he still has to go. To allow his mind to deviate, even for just a second, would mean death. All his attention, all his *personal power*, must be given totally to the act of survival.

> *EVERYTHING IN LIFE IS BUT A CHALLENGE. CHALLENGES CAN NEVER BE GOOD OR BAD; WE MAKE OF OUR CHALLENGES WHAT WE WILL.*

The soldier's chances of survival are practically nil, and this he acknowledges. Yet he also knows that had he never entered this terrain he certainly would have died at the hands of his enemy. Now, having chosen this route, hopelessness has given way to challenge. Only one small mistake is needed for the soldier to forfeit his life. Faced with such impossible odds, the soldier would be a fool if he did not consider himself already dead. However, for the warrior to indulge in the luxury of bemoaning his fate would be to spend precious *personal power* and to waste his challenge. The real challenge facing him is not how to survive, but rather how much time he can win, how far he can go before he dies.

A WARRIOR LIVES BY CHALLENGE.

THE AVERAGE MAN SEES EVERYTHING IN HIS LIFE AS EITHER A BLESSING OR A CURSE; THE WARRIOR SEES EVERYTHING AS A CHALLENGE.

Looking at the soldier, one could argue that the terrain of landmines was a blessing because his enemies would not follow him into that area. Alternatively, one could say that he was cursed with bad luck in having to traverse such a dangerous place in trying to escape from his enemies. This is typical of most occurrences in our lives. However, situations such as these do not lend themselves to rationalization. Any situation is merely what you wish to make of it, and as important as the meaning you attach to it.

ANY SITUATION IN LIFE IS NEUTRAL. WE MAKE IT POSITIVE OR NEGATIVE ACCORDING TO THE MEANING WE ATTACH TO IT. MEANING, THOUGH, DOES NOT ALTER THE CONTENT OF A SITUATION; THEREFORE MEANINGS SERVE ONLY TO PLACATE THE REASON.

From our example it is clear that the soldier is not in a position to rationalize about his situation, and therefore meanings no longer have any significance for him.

IT IS INSANITY FOR ANY MAN TO WISH FOR A DIFFERENT LIFE TO THE ONE HE HAS. SUCH WISHES ARE BASED UPON THE DEMENTED IDEA THAT COWARDICE OR LAZINESS, OR BOTH, ARE HONOURABLE PURSUITS.

If the soldier were to start dreaming about being somewhere else, or to wish for a better situation, he would only be allowing his mind to deviate from the challenge at hand. Clearly this would be a most foolish act, courting disaster. In this challenge the soldier's life has become more important than fanciful wishes. By keeping his wits about him, every step taken safely extends the soldier's tenuous existence one moment longer.

To believe that we have all the time in the world is not only stupid, but also takes away our appreciation of life, for where there is no awareness of death, boredom and discontent quickly set in. The warrior knows that his death is constantly stalking him; therefore whatever time he has is a most priceless gift. Knowing that his time cannot last, the warrior savours his gift to the full, and enjoys every moment of this precious time. This is what is known as *living on the edge*.

A MAN CAN ONLY BE SURPRISED IF HE HAS NOT TAKEN THE UNEXPECTED INTO ACCOUNT. BECAUSE SURPRISE DRAINS PERSONAL POWER, A WARRIOR MUST INCLUDE THE UNEXPECTED IN HIS DECISIONS. THIS MEANS THAT A WARRIOR LIVES ON THE EDGE. A WARRIOR CAN LIVE ON THE EDGE BECAUSE HE IS HUMBLE AND FULLY AWARE.

Generally speaking, man is very seldom fully aware, for he spends most of his life dreaming either of the past or of the future and thus rarely notices the present. It is therefore not so strange that he is frequently caught off guard, and so often lands himself in trouble. Furthermore, to be unaware of the present and the challenges it bring us is gross arrogance and conceit. By ignoring the present we imply that we do not care for the precious gift of life, preferring instead our daydreams.

Such an attitude is contrary to the mood of a warrior, because a warrior is a being who has learned the true value of life. Acknowledging this value, the warrior can see what a wonderful privilege it is to be alive.

Realising that he has nothing to offer in return for this incredible gift, he offers the only thing he has, namely his full appreciation. Humbled by the poverty of his human resources, the only way in which a warrior can justify the awesome gift of life is by treasuring every aspect of it in full awareness.

Full awareness naturally also includes anticipating the unexpected, because the warrior knows he is living in a fluid universe pervaded by the unpredictable quirks of *power*. Therefore, whenever a warrior has to make a decision, he will always do so taking into account the fact that he does not presume to know beforehand what the outcome of his decision will be. By accepting the unknown the warrior never falls into the trap of assuming that he does not need to be fully aware.

Savoured in full awareness, the warrior's life is never empty or boring, but instead filled with a never-ending sequence of wondrous events, each leading him into a new adventure, a new challenge. Each new challenge is for him a breath-taking experience, because in living on the very edge of life the warrior acknowledges the fine line between annihilation and survival. For the average man to live on the edge is tantamount to having to endure a devastating nightmare; for the warrior it is a chance he embraces gladly, because living on the edge is for him an expression of his deep appreciation and respect for life.

A WARRIOR ACCEPTS THE CHALLENGES OF LIFE IN TRUE HUMILITY. NO MATTER WHAT HIS DESTINY MAY BE, IT CAN NEVER BE A CAUSE FOR DISCONTENT, BUT A LIVING CHALLENGE WHICH IT IS HIS PRIVILEGE TO SURMOUNT.

The only reason why man hates the thought of living on the edge is because he insists on holding onto the idea that his life is not what he feels it should be. Being plagued all too frequently by feelings of discontent and bitterness man constantly hopes to change his life into what he imagines he would like it to be. In order to maintain these hopes man must believe in some future time in which he will be able to materialise his wishes. Thinking in this way, it is not so surprising that man should abhor the thought of living on the edge, for the concept, and all that it entails, threatens his entire view of the world, filling him with an overpowering sense of insecurity and doom.

At the bottom of man's inability to accept his life for what it is lies his assumption that he knows better than the forces which guide us all throughout life. What never occurs to man is that there is no way in which he can possibly justify such a belief, for none of us has the necessary insight to judge our own destiny. Without this insight, assumptions of this nature must inevitably be based upon arrogance and *reason*.

AVERAGE MAN IS ARROGANT, BECAUSE HE IS EVER IMPRESSED BY REASON AND ALWAYS BOWS HIS HEAD TO IT.

REASON MAKES US BELIEVE THAT OUR CHALLENGES IN LIFE ARE TO BE AVOIDED AT ALL COSTS. THIS IS TO BE A COWARD WHO DOES NOT HAVE THE SELF-RESPECT NEEDED IN ORDER TO HONOUR THE MARVELLOUS GIFT OF LIFE.

The warrior can never assume the arrogance that man generally regards as his right, for not only is the warrior much too humble, but he also does not award reason the same respect as the average man. In this, the warrior is far more *reasonable* than average man, because to regard reason as granting one carte blanche to avoid the challenges of life is a most *unreasonable* act. The warrior uses his reason merely to guide him into experiencing life to its full, and not as an excuse to run away from his challenges.

> *THERE EXISTS A VAST DIFFERENCE BETWEEN ARROGANCE AND HUMILITY. ARROGANCE IS BASED UPON THE ASSUMPTION THAT ONE IS SUPERIOR TO SOMEONE OR SOMETHING ELSE. HUMILITY IS BASED UPON THE KNOWLEDGE THAT ONE IS NOT ELEVATED ABOVE OR MORE IMPORTANT THAN ANYTHING ELSE. BUT MAN REGARDS HIMSELF AS BEING HUMBLE WHEN HE UPHOLDS WHAT HE TERMS RESPECT FOR A SUPERIOR; THEREFORE IN HIS CONCEIT HE WORSHIPS ARROGANCE.*

The only time a man will face a challenge is when reason assures him that he will come out on top. It is the rare man indeed who will willingly undertake a task which he thinks might be to his detriment. Such reasoning is always founded in the belief that not to succeed is a disgrace, and is to become less in the eyes of one's fellow men. This, in turn, presupposes that one is somehow elevated in the first place, because only if one has a position of importance can one possibly lose it.

Unlike average man, the warrior knows that he is neither more important nor less important than anything else. He knows this by virtue of the fact that he is alive. The priceless gift of life with which he has been endowed is the same life-force as that bestowed upon a king, a beggar and an insect. Such knowledge is very sobering indeed, and it is only the conceited fool who will fail to be humbled by this fact. The warrior takes no part in arrogance, but through his humility he has a profound respect for all of life, no matter if that life is himself, a king, a beggar, an animal, a plant, an insect or an atom.

Man often confuses humility with arrogance and therefore has no real respect for life. Think of the soldier fleeing for his life. Would you have acted differently to the soldier had you been in his position? Faced with certain death you would have taken your chances just as he did. Yet in daily life man loves to complain, and through this to indulge in feelings of helplessness. Essentially there is nothing wrong in feeling helpless, but to indulge in this feeling is a very different kettle of fish. If the soldier had merely indulged in his feeling of helplessness he would have been a dead soldier.

Indulging in a sense of helplessness is habitual for mankind, and is usually regarded as the sign of a humble man. By declaring that he is helpless in a given situation a man always manages to manipulate others into shouldering his responsibility for him. Considering that there are always those who are looking for an opportunity to prove themselves, a helpless man never wants for a helping hand. Helplessness is obviously then a most convenient tool to use whenever faced with some challenge which is either feared or despised. The fact that people are normally willing to assist a helpless man does not change the fact that such a man is merely manipulating others to his own advantage. There is nothing humble about manipulation. On the contrary, it is arrogant.

Situations in which help is genuinely called for are mostly few and far between, and never entail another person having to shoulder someone else's responsibility. This shifting around of responsibility is always manipulation, and is the most powerful way in which man maintains the so-called order of social conditioning.

> *IN AN EMERGENCY, OLD HABITS ARE ALWAYS A MOST WELCOME REFUGE, EVEN IF WE NORMALLY HATE THEM.*

In order to avoid the trap of his old habits, and especially to avoid indulging in the feeling of being helpless, the warrior adopts the stance which has been explained briefly in Chapter Two.

WHENEVER FACED WITH THE UNKNOWN, THE WARRIOR BEHAVES AS IF NOTHING UNTOWARD HAS HAPPENED. KNOWING THAT THE WORLD IS NOT WHAT IT APPEARS TO BE, THE WARRIOR DOES NOT BELIEVE FOR THE SAKE OF BELIEVING, AND YET HE ACKNOWLEDGES EVERYTHING AT FACE VALUE. THEREFORE THE WARRIOR ACKNOWLEDGES WITHOUT ACKNOWLEDGING, AND IGNORES WITHOUT IGNORING. THE WARRIOR NEVER ASSUMES UNDERSTANDING, NOR DOES HE ASSUME IGNORANCE. INSTEAD HE BEHAVES AS IF HE IS IN CONTROL, EVEN THOUGH HE MAY BE THOROUGHLY BEWILDERED AND FRIGHTENED. BY ADOPTING THIS STANCE THE WARRIOR AVOIDS OBSESSION.

In order to grasp all this more fully let us return to our example of the soldier. If we did not know the circumstances in which this soldier finds himself we would observe a completely different scenario.

What we would see is a soldier who is apparently taking a slow walk through a rough terrain. From his actions we can deduce that he is looking for something on the ground or perhaps in the grass. In fact, the soldier is the picture of calm concentration, utterly absorbed in his search. Looking at him, one gets the impression that he has all the time in the world, and judging by his slow and careful movements, one would never suspect him to be a desperate man fleeing for his life. This is what is meant by a warrior *behaving as if nothing untoward has happened* – this is his *control.*

If the soldier believed that there was no chance of escaping, he would not have taken his chances to begin with. It was imperative for the soldier to *acknowledge the face value* of his situation, because if he had not fled into that terrain his enemies would have caught up with him. But having entered that deadly area, he is likely to die anyway. In others words, the soldier had to acknowledge that not to act would mean death, but to act would also more than likely mean death.

In doing this, the soldier had to believe that he was going to die at the hands of his enemies. Likewise, in order to pick his way between the landmines safely, he also had to believe in the possibility of stepping on a landmine and being blown to shreds. Yet, although the soldier acknowledged fully the presence of death, he did not just give up in despair. To have given up would have been to yield meekly to death, something no true warrior would ever consider doing.

> *A WARRIOR NEVER CEDES HIS PERSONAL POWER TO ANYTHING, NOT EVEN TO HIS DEATH.*

Instead of feeling helpless the soldier took his chances, slim as they were, and entered a hell-hole. Through his actions the soldier acknowledged death but did not surrender to it. This is what is meant by ***a warrior acknowledges without acknowledging, and ignores without ignoring.***

> *IN THE FACE OF CERTAIN DEATH NOTHING MATTERS ANY MORE BECAUSE THE WORST IS ALREADY AT HAND. BY ACCEPTING DEATH AS AN INHERENT FACTOR OF LIFE, THE WARRIOR IS ALWAYS CALM AND LUCID.*

The soldier has no notion of what the outcome of his actions will be, but this is in no way his concern. Taking responsibility for his situation, the soldier chooses the only viable option open to him. In this, he acts impeccably and therefore he knows, without having to deliberate upon it, that the outcome of his actions is not in his hands. The only thing he can do is to give that fatal terrain his full awareness. This means that the warrior ***is not assuming that he understands*** what is taking place, but neither does he ignore the situation. The warrior merely acts impeccably upon the knowledge available to him in that moment.

THE IMPECCABILITY OF A WARRIOR DOES NOT ALLOW HIM TO BECOME OBSESSED WITH THE POSSIBLE OUTCOME OF HIS ACTIONS. WINNING OR LOSING IS NOT IN ANY WAY HIS CONCERN – HE IS MERELY ABSORBED IN THE CHALLENGE OF THE MOMENT.

TO BECOME OBSESSED IS TO LOSE CONTROL, SOMETHING A WARRIOR CANNOT AFFORD TO DO, FOR A WARRIOR MUST BE CALM AND ALWAYS KEEP HIS WITS ABOUT HIM.

By acting in this way the soldier is *behaving as if he is in control*, and to see him in action one would never believe that he may be *thoroughly bewildered and frightened*. Through his impeccable behaviour the warrior avoids the deadly trap of obsession. To become obsessed with anything is tantamount to being defeated before one has even entered the battle.

Had the soldier been obsessed with staying alive he would have panicked and died anyway. Had he been obsessed with escaping he would have tried to cross the terrain too quickly and consequently would have killed himself. Not being obsessed either with his fear of death or with his hope of escape, the soldier in effect acknowledged both, and neither. This is a fine state of mind and the very core of a warrior's condition. For the average man such a condition is a nightmare, but for the warrior, who lives by challenge, even a nightmare is but a challenge worthy of his finest behaviour.

IT IS THE PRIME REQUISITE OF A WARRIOR'S BEING THAT HIS CONTROL MUST BE IMPECCABLE; THEREFORE HE NEVER ALLOWS ANYTHING TO AFFECT HIM. A WARRIOR MAY BE STARING DEATH IN THE FACE, BUT HIS ACTIONS WILL REVEAL NOTHING.

The soldier's only hope of escape is to embrace the presence of death and to allow that presence to guide him into the unfoldment of his destiny. If it is his destiny to live, the presence of death will guide him safely between the landmines and away from his enemies. At the same time the threat of death will keep the soldier's enemies from pursuing him into that area. If, on the other hand, it is the soldier's destiny to die, then at least he will die an impeccable death and not the miserable death of a whimpering coward.

All of us must one day die. If we are to die tomorrow, or next year, then why not today, right now? In man's fear of death he will avoid it at all costs, even at the expense of an honourable life. Although the warrior too fears death, he nevertheless also knows it to be his constant companion, and his best advisor. Therefore, the warrior does not try to avoid death, but knows that as long as he treats it with the utmost respect it will guide him into living an impeccable life which is filled with richness, *power* and the excitement of challenge.

> *HAVING WITNESSED THE VERY ESSENCE OF LIFE AND DEATH, THERE IS NOTHING IN THIS WORLD WHICH A WARRIOR CANNOT CONTEND WITH, ALTHOUGH TO JUDGE FROM HIS BEHAVIOUR ONE WOULD NEVER SUSPECT THIS.*

Toltecs claim that to live the impeccable life of a warrior is the only justification for man being endowed with the priceless gift of life. This claim they can make honestly and without arrogance or conceit, because they have come to recognize the true value of both life and death. Only those who are truly humble can understand that life is not more important than death. Without death the value of life would fade into total insignificance.

ELEPHANT

Gentle giant - he who is warrior, friend and pillar of strength.

'... an old woman, symbol for the tonal of man, ugly and emaciated from ages of neglect, waits within the flat-topped mountain above the Cape of Storms, dreaming of the day when the young elephant will free her, and with his love and care, nurse her back to her former strength and beauty - she who is the mother of all'.

Extract from an old African myth.

(Pencil drawing: Susan Emily)

Susan Emily

CHAPTER SIX

THE PREDILECTION OF THE WARRIOR

TIME IS THE ESSENCE OF IMPECCABILITY. IT IS ONLY THE SENSE OF MORTALITY WHICH ENGENDERS IN MAN THE DESIRE TO ACT IMPECCABLY.

In observing warriors one can easily be led to believe that they are extremely self-confident people. However, it should be realised that there is an enormous difference between what man generally terms *self-confidence* and the deeper implications of the term. This term is important in that it clarifies the difference between two distinct concepts, namely *impeccability* and *perfection*. It is not easy to define impeccability without getting caught up in the concept of perfection, and yet there is a fine distinction between the two. This distinction lies in the difference between *arrogance* and *humility*, two further concepts which can only be understood through the term self-confidence. If we are to come to grips with the Warrior's Path these terms must be carefully defined.

SELF-CONFIDENCE, AS IT IS GENERALLY UNDERSTOOD, IMPLIES ARROGANT PRESUMPTION; HUMILITY IMPLIES BEING IMPECCABLE IN ONE'S ACTIONS AND FEELINGS.

In order to grasp this we must realise that whenever average man is certain of his fellow man's approval he acts with a great deal of assurance and calls this self-confidence. However, the moment the man senses that his fellow man is not in agreement with him he suddenly lacks his previous bravado. This happens, firstly, because of man's arrogance in persisting in his belief that one person can be more important than another, and secondly, because man is dependant upon his fellow man's approval in order to maintain his sense of self-importance.

Since the warrior does not regard himself as being more important or less important than his fellow man, it does not matter to him if he loses face in the eyes of his fellow men. In other words, the warrior does not strive to be self-important and therefore does not care about public approval. This freedom from having to seek approval is true humility. Since he no longer has to fear the impact his actions may have upon his sense of self-importance, the warrior's only consideration is to act upon his own knowledge to the very best of his ability. Accordingly, a warrior understands self-confidence to mean *confidence in one's own ability to act like an impeccable warrior.*

It is obvious how different these two approaches are, and yet people often make the mistake of confusing the act of seeking approval with self-confidence. In seeking approval from his fellow men, man very rarely acts freely upon his own knowledge. To avoid acting according to one's own knowledge merely to win the favour of someone else, is to be unimpeccable.

IMPECCABILITY IS TO ACT TO THE VERY BEST OF YOUR ABILITY UPON WHATEVER KNOWLEDGE HAPPENS TO BE AVAILABLE TO YOU AT ANY GIVEN MOMENT.

TIME IS THE ESSENCE OF IMPECCABILITY; IT IS ONLY THE SENSE OF MORTALITY WHICH ENGENDERS IN MAN THE DESIRE TO ACT IMPECCABLY.

When man is called upon to consider the concept of impeccability he usually cannot distinguish between perfection and impeccability. However, perfection is not at all the same as impeccability. To strive for perfection has the hidden motive of wanting to be the best. There is nothing wrong with this provided that one does not want to be the best merely to gain recognition or approval from one's fellow men. In addition, perfection usually means that a great deal of time and energy is spent in trying to achieve one's goal. The man who is striving for perfection usually makes the mistake of assuming that he has all the time in the world. Such a man's motto is: 'If at first I don't succeed, then I'll try again.'

Just as in the case of wanting to be the best, there is also nothing wrong with repetition as such, because most acts in life can only be perfected through constant practice and repetition. The problem here arises from the idea of having unlimited time in which to keep on trying, because unless multiple attempts are imbued with a sense of urgency they inevitably result in timidity. A timid man rarely, if ever, gives of his ultimate best.

TO ACHIEVE ABSOLUTE PERFECTION IS POSSIBLE ONLY UNDER EXTRAORDINARY CONDITIONS. THE AIM OF THE WARRIOR IS TO ACHIEVE AS MUCH PERFECTION AS HE IS CAPABLE OF IN ANY GIVEN SITUATION.

The warrior approaches the concept of perfection in a very different manner to the average man. Knowing that death is stalking him, the warrior is fully aware that he will not necessarily have the time to try again if at first he fails. This is something which all actors understand very well. Once the curtain has been raised, the actor has only one chance to prove himself worthy. If he makes a mess of his only chance, the future of his career hangs in the balance. Similarly, the warrior acknowledges that the best in life is never repeated. If there are repetitions then the original impact is lost, and what is left is but second choice. In order to clarify this, let us take the example of recorded music as opposed to a live performance.

Recorded music is a good substitute for a live performance, but irrespective of how fine the recording is, it remains a substitute which can never replace live music. In a live performance there is an exchange of vibrant energy between artist and audience, and there is an excitement generated by the uncertainty involved. A live performance which has been impeccably presented is always infinitely more exhilarating than a perfect recording. The real difference lies in the possibility that anything can go wrong during a performance and, as a result, both artist and audience are on edge and wide awake. There is always at the end of a performance a strange mixture of consuming happiness and heart-felt relief when all has gone well. This feeling can never be captured by listening to a recording, simply because there is not the edge which comes from having only one chance.

In this respect the warrior is an artist in his own lifestyle. The warrior cannot claim the luxury of being confused or uncertain, because the presence of death does not allow him the time in which to indulge in sloppy performances. A warrior sees each act as being possibly his last on earth, and therefore that act must be the very best he can perform. This does not imply that the warrior will necessarily be perfect in his actions; instead he strives to make them as perfect as he possibly can in that one chance. In this way his actions take on a vibrant quality of total awareness mixed with that deep poignancy which comes from the knowledge that this particular moment will never again be repeated.

Every moment in our lives passes. No moment can ever be called back when it has gone, and no opportunity can ever be repeated in the true sense of the word. In the example of the musician we can see that even if he repeated the same performance a hundred times, no two performances would ever be identical. Life never repeats itself – only a mechanical recording can be classified as being an identical repetition.

Since no moment in life can be repeated, it makes little sense to fritter away time by engaging in actions which are not of our best. It is because people do just this that they live lives filled with regrets, lament over an ill-spent youth, or grieve for the opportunities lost in a broken relationship. None of us is immortal, and none of us knows where or when we will encounter our death. From the moment we are born death begins to stalk us. In the presence of death any act, regardless of size or significance, can be one's last. Death can find one doing the shopping, driving one's car, eating a meal, spending time with a loved one, or simply watching a beautiful sunset. If any act is going to be one's last on earth, then it makes sense that it should be the finest of all one's actions, and that one should savour every detail of those last few moments.

To live one's life in the knowledge that every moment, that every act, matters, is to fill one's life with uncountable riches and to imbue all one's actions with that quality termed impeccability. It does not matter to the impeccable warrior that his life or his actions may be less than perfect. In living his life to the full, and in performing each action to the best of his ability, the warrior has no regrets and suffers no remorse. A life lived in this way is rich in joy and wonder, because there are no missed opportunites and no lost moments of pleasure.

Man's relentless pursuit of perfection in its countless different guises is the greatest cause of unhappiness in the world. Man mostly postpones his pleasure in life, suspends it until such time as he has the perfect career, the perfect home or the perfect bank balance. In his pursuit of perfection man never fully enjoys the present moment, or his present situation, and therefore rarely gives of his best. Instead man lives a life which is only vaguely happy, filled as it is with undesired experiences only partially perceived, and half-hearted actions which are less than impeccable.

PERFECTION IS A STUPID WASTE OF TIME AND PERSONAL POWER, WHEREAS IMPECCABILITY REPLENISHES PERSONAL POWER.

The reason why man places so much importance upon

perfection is because he enjoys the idea of being superior to his fellow man. As a result, people generally spend an inordinate amount of time thinking about perfection in one way or another. This excessive reflection gives rise to a great many fears and doubts based upon feelings of inadequacy. Man justifies these negative feelings by regarding them as being the sign of a thinking man – one who has deep insight, and thus one who can see all sides of a situation. This, however, is sadly very far from the truth because such a man is not thinking in the proper sense of the word, but merely indulging in fears and doubts and consequently dithering away precious time and opportunity.

TRUE THINKING IS INSTANTANEOUS; ONLY TRIVIALITIES BASED UPON SELF-IMPORTANCE TAKE TIME TO CIRCLE THROUGH THE MIND.

Through social conditioning man has grown to accept that to strive for perfection is the ultimate goal of mankind, and his reason assures him that to indulge in doubts and confusion is only normal. And so, man looks around him and, seeing that his fellow man thinks the same, he feels self-assured and confident. Seeking approval from his reason as well as his fellow men, average man is caught in a vicious circle of his own making. Before such a man can break out of this circle he must be willing to take his chances and to forfeit approval, especially approval from his rational mind.

THE WARRIOR CANNOT UPHOLD THE LOGIC OF REASON BECAUSE HE KNOWS THAT DEATH LEAVES NO ROOM FOR REASONABLE ASSUMPTIONS. THEREFORE THE WARRIOR IS ALWAYS READY TO GRAB HIS FLEETING MOMENT OF CHANCE.

Reason is man's biggest downfall. When it comes to having to take his chances, man's reason will inevitably intervene with all manner of doubts and fears. Reason has no sense of adventure and no sense of humour. Instead it is a dour and jealous faculty. Reason is so jealous of attention that it cannot even tolerate man taking notice of his other faculties, such as feeling or intuition. Whenever reason finds its authority being threatened, it will always resort to the incomprehensible act of trying to make man admit to defeat, normally through confusion.

By throwing up a fog of confusion, man's reason usually succeeds in forcing him to adhere to the so-called reasonable approach. This inevitably terminates in man becoming timid and frightened, and under such conditions he never takes his chances. What man never realises is that thanks to his reason he always misses the boat by choosing the safe way out. It is a strange quirk of reason that it will rather admit defeat than relinquish its control. Therefore the reasonable man will always seek excuses for not acting rather than seize his fleeting moment of chance.

AVERAGE MAN IS EVER SEEKING REFUGE IN FAILURE SO THAT HE CAN SURRENDER ON THE TERMS OF HIS REASON, BUT IT IS NOT POSSIBLE TO FAKE FAILURE OR TRIUMPH.

What man usually terms failure is not true failure at all, but simply an excuse for shying away from a challenge which is not to his reason's liking. The only way to circumvent the control of reason is to remember that reason is only powerful as long as one upholds the idea that one's view of the world is reality. Stop your view of the world and reason meekly retires to its proper place. Reason cannot behave in a superior fashion if one does not adhere to social conditioning, because man's reason is completely programmed by his social conditioning. However, as we have already seen, to stop one's view of the world and to break out of one's social conditioning is only possible if one lives like a warrior.

NO MAN IS BORN A WARRIOR, NOR IS HE BORN A REASONING BEING – WE CHOOSE TO BECOME EITHER ONE OR THE OTHER.

In order to become a warrior, one must be prepared to take one's chances and fight for one's freedom. There is no other way.

ONE CANNOT BECOME A WARRIOR SIMPLY BY WISHING TO DO SO. TO BECOME A WARRIOR IS THE STRUGGLE OF A LIFETIME.

The warrior is not immune to the problems of the average man. In his struggle to be impeccable there are many times when even the warrior succumbs to doubt and fear, insecurity, feelings of helplessness, and above all, loneliness. However, the warrior knows that all these feelings are but moods which spur him on to even greater heights, and so he plumbs their depths in order to find their deeper meanings. Unfortunately though, average man never makes the effort to question the true validity of his moods, but merely accepts them at face value.

SHOULD A WARRIOR FEEL THE NEED TO BE COMFORTED, HE SIMPLY CHOOSES ANYONE OR ANYTHING, BE IT A FRIEND, DOG, OR MOUNTAIN, TO WHOM HE EXPRESSES HIS INNERMOST FEELINGS. IT DOES NOT MATTER TO THE WARRIOR IF HE IS NOT ANSWERED, OR IF HE IS NOT HEARD, BECAUSE THE WARRIOR IS NOT SEEKING TO BE UNDERSTOOD OR HELPED – BY VERBALISING HIS FEELINGS HE IS MERELY RELEASING THE PRESSURE OF HIS BATTLE.

Such is the predilection of a warrior, and such is the impeccability of his spirit.

However, when the average man feels the need to be comforted, he is invariably looking for confirmation of his view of the world. On such occasions man is usually faced with a challenge he feels he cannot cope with and so turns to someone whom he is fairly certain will agree with him. Feeling inadequate, he tries to convince his listener that there is no point in his trying to fight. In this way, he seeks to impress upon his friend that he wishes to be encouraged to admit to defeat and to throw in the towel. Should his friend agree with him, the man feels confident that he has the right to surrender on his own terms, rather than keep on trying.

The prime requirement for walking the Warrior's Path is the state of impeccability, but to achieve this we must sacrifice our view of the world. The principal constituent of this view is the belief that we have unlimited time on this earth. In this, reason is ever leading us astray, because reason delights in making us believe that it understands everything, and has it all under control. Yet there is very little to understand other than the fact that we all have incredible abilities and awesome potentials which never surface unless a sword is dangling overhead.

Accordingly, the warrior chooses to live by challenge and acknowledges the fact that he cannot afford to behave like an immortal being. The warrior does not waste his time in complaining about his life, nor does he waste his *personal power* in blaming others. Living on the very edge of life the warrior is always ready to seize his fleeting moment of chance and to claim his *power*. The warrior is an impeccable being fighting for his freedom, and in his struggle he sees life for what it truly is. For the warrior, life is a short but exhilarating detour in this marvellously beautiful world – an extravagant detour rich in challenge and opportunity, and one in which he is also given everything he needs in order to make his journey one of joy and success.

Today the whole of humanity stands on the threshold of a new era. Consequently you have been guided to this book by those powers which guide the life and death of every living being on this earth. In accordance with the ancient prophecy I have revealed within this book knowledge which has never before been openly revealed to anyone other than a selected few. By virtue of this you can no longer plead ignorance. Right now the *Spirit* * is knocking upon your door. You can open the door if you wish, or you may ignore the knock. You can if you wish seize your fleeting moment of chance and go with the *Spirit*, or you can return to your present existence if that is what your heart is telling you to do.

However, before making your decision, ask yourself this question: '*Does my path have a heart*?'

I cannot possibly answer this question for you, nor can I truly express the poignancy of all that has to be imparted at this point. Instead, I offer you the moving words of Walter de la Mare. In his poem, *The Listeners*, de la Mare expresses the mood and intensity of this moment most profoundly.

'Is there anybody there ?' said the Traveller,
Knocking on the moonlit door;
And his horse in the silence champed the grasses
Of the forest's ferny floor:
And a bird flew up out of the turret,
Above the Traveller's head:
And he smote upon the door again a second time;
'Is there anybody there ?' he said.
But no one descended to the Traveller;
No head from the leaf-fringed sill
Leaned over and looked into his grey eyes,
Where he stood perplexed and still.
But only a host of phantom listeners

---

* *The nagal or that ineffable Presence which permeates the entire manifested universe, but which also exists beyond it; the Unspeakable or that great void in which the manifested universe is contained during any one of its periodic appearances.*

That dwelt in the lone house then
Stood listening in the quiet of the moonlight
To that voice from the world of men:
Stood thronging the faint moonbeams on the dark stair,
That goes down to the empty hall,
Hearkening in an air stirred and shaken
By the lonely Traveller's call.
And he felt in his heart their strangeness,
Their stillness answering his cry,
While his horse moved, cropping the dark turf,
'Neath the starred and leafy sky;
For he suddenly smote on the door, even
Louder, and lifted his head:-
'Tell them I came, and no one answered,
That I kept my word,' he said.
Never the least stir made the listeners,
Though every word he spake
Fell echoing through the shadowiness of the still house
From the one man left awake:
Ay, they heard his foot upon the stirrup,
And the sound of iron on stone,
And how the silence surged softly backward,
When the plunging hoofs were gone. [1]

Should you decide that your present path offers you the fulfilment you desire, then there is no need for you to open the door. Put this book quietly out of your mind, but remember one thing – the *Spirit* comes only once in the life of every man. Life does not permit itself to be repeated for this would cause stagnation. To believe that there will be time to catch up later is a fool's game, because after the *Spirit* has knocked it waits but a moment before it leaves. In this respect man's only constant companion throughout life is death, who of course offers us no guarantees on life.

If, on the other hand, you should choose to answer the knock upon your door, then remember that you will be choosing a path of no return. Once one embarks upon the Path of Freedom one's life becomes irrevocably changed, and that change does not permit one to hold onto one's previous existence. Once again I can do no better here than to refer you to the final verse of T. S. Eliot's poem, *Journey of the Magi*.

> *'We returned to our places, these Kingdoms,*
> *But no longer at ease here, in the old dispensation,*
> *With an alien people clutching their gods.*
> *I should be glad of another death'.* [2]

PART THREE

The Teachings:
PRACTICAL TECHNIQUES

DRAGON

'... with focused intent shall they divide the world in two, so that light and darkness shall stand fully revealed. Then shall the Spear of Destiny fly true once more, and the Sword of Power shall again ring with the One Truth and flash forth the blue flame of the One Power.'

Extract from the prophecies of The Nameless One.

(Ink drawing: Susan Emily)

Susan Emily

CHAPTER SEVEN

WORKING WITH EMOTION AND INTENT

Before we can launch into the practical techniques such as *recapitulation* and *not-doing*, we first need to clarify a few of the key concepts touched upon earlier. In this respect it is of paramount importance to bear in mind that the Warrior's Path is a practical path. This implies, firstly, that the teachings must be put into practice if they are to benefit the reader, and secondly, that the only true knowledge is that which arises out of personal experience. This point is stressed again here because so often apprentices fall into the trap of believing that the practical exercises are sufficient in themselves – they are not. All of the teachings are necessary, and unless the apprentice endeavours to put every one of the various concepts into practice he will not succeed upon the Warrior's Path. This is especially true with regard to the teachings on *emotion* and *intent*.

The knowledge which the warrior seeks is the product of perception, namely *power*; but perception can only take place within the occurrences of daily life. Such perception will obviously be unique to every individual, and therefore the knowledge gained from an experience will naturally also be unique. After only a little practice the individual quickly realises that the greater portion of this knowledge cannot be properly verbalized, even though it may have been understood. It is for this reason that Toltecs have always maintained that the *true teachings* have never been, and can never be, written down or notated in any form whatsoever.

Contrary to popular belief, all knowledge arises on the left side and, as such, is irrational. The only activity which takes place on the right side is the computation and structuring of knowledge gained on the left side, and the arrangement of information gathered from theory. It should always be remembered that the left side is irrational and therefore does not conform to the linear and sequential thought patterns experienced in normal awareness, that is, the right side. Consequently, it is impossible to verbalize the left side accurately – we can at best verbalize our experiences of the left side; or in other words, we can express and describe what we have witnessed on the left side, but this expression will only be a logical interpretation of knowledge which is beyond the scope of words, since words by their very nature demand a linear and sequential mode in order to be coherent.

There is always a great deal of confusion within the new apprentice as to the true nature and manifestation of left side awareness. Yet there is nothing mysterious about left side awareness, or heightened awareness, as it is sometimes referred to. All of mankind is familiar with it, although they never fully identify or understand it. Let us therefore expand on this point a little more for the sake of clarity. To do this we must review the Truths of Awareness, which for convenience are repeated here.

THE TRUTHS OF AWARENESS

1. The universe consists of an infinite number of energy fields resembling threads of light.

2. These threadlike energy fields radiate from a source of unimaginable dimensions metaphorically called the Eagle. As such these energy fields are known as the Eagle's Emanations.

3. Human beings are likewise composed of the same infinite number of these threadlike energy fields which manifest in the shape of a large luminous egg. The height of this egg is equal to the length of a man's body with his arms fully extended above his head on the vertical axis, and its width is that of a man with his arms extended outwards from the centre of his body along the horizontal axis. This egg is known as the cocoon of man.

4. Only a small group of the energy fields inside the cocoon are lit up at any one time by a brilliant point of light located on the surface of the cocoon.

5. Perception takes place when the energy fields which are illuminated by the point of light extend their light to illuminate corresponding energy fields outside the cocoon. This point of light is termed the point where perception is assembled, normally abbreviated to the assemblage point.

6. It is possible to shift the assemblage point to any other position on the surface of the cocoon, or even into its interior. Because the assemblage point illuminates any energy fields with which it comes into contact, the new energy fields it illuminates as a result of such shifting constitute therefore a new perception. It is this new level of perception that is known as ***seeing****.*

7. When the assemblage point shifts sufficiently far a totally new world is perceived, which is as real as the one man normally perceives.

8. There is a mysterious force known as ***intent*** *which exists throughout the entire universe. It is this force which brings about perception, for it is* ***intent*** *which,* *firstly, aligns the energy fields, and secondly, causes awareness of that alignment.*

9. The goal of warriors is to experience all possible perceptions available to man. This constitutes what is known as ***Total Awareness****, inherent within which is an alternate way of dying.*

These nine precepts form the cornerstone of the Toltec Teachings. Everything warriors understand and do is based upon these fundamental precepts. Therefore these truths should be studied until they are fully understood, and then thoroughly internalized. Without this ABC of the Toltec Path the teachings degenerate into a useless collection of empty intellectualisms.

A point which should be remembered with regard to the Truths of Awareness is that man is the microcosm of the macrocosm – that is, man is an exact replica in miniature of the entire universe. Within the universe there are seven great bands of interrelated energy fields which each manifest in turn as seven sub-bands. This is true also of man. Stretching across several of these great bands within the cocoon of man are a medley of sub-bands forming a particular collection of energy fields. This collection constitutes that quality of awareness which is identified as being peculiarly *human*.

This medley of sub-bands is most confusing to anyone other than the experienced seer, and is therefore referred to quite simply as the *Band of Man*. However, because the majority of possible perceptions within the Band of Man are beyond man's normal experience and therefore beyond his normal awareness, they are technically referred to as the *unknown*.

In the Toltec teachings normal awareness is known as the First Attention, that is, the right side. The left side is known as the Second Attention. The First Attention is defined as being *all the possible permutations of perception within the 'normal' position of the assemblage point.* In this respect the average man, not having a fluid assemblage point, always uses only one of the possible permutations available within normal awareness, and terms this the *known*. On the other hand, a warrior, having achieved a fluid assemblage point, unfolds *all* of the possible permutations of the First Attention, and terms this *clarity* or *sobriety*.

The Second Attention, or left side, is *the totality of all possible permutations of perception which become available whenever the assemblage point shifts anywhere within the Band of Man*, that is, within the scope of those energy fields which constitute the true human experience. Much confusion will be avoided later if at this point it is realised that these energy fields must obviously also include those of the animal kingdom, of which man is a species.

Logical thought, with its linear quality, is only possible under the impact of reason. However, reason can only operate in normal awareness, because it is only when the assemblage point aligns those particular energy fields which constitute the First Attention that thought can flow in a linear and sequential fashion. This is both the peculiarity and the advantage of the First Attention. Whenever the assemblage point aligns energy fields which are not part of the First Attention, linear thought ceases, and knowledge flows in an irrational pattern in which sequence, and therefore also time, has no bearing.

Whenever knowledge flows in an irrational manner in which there is no apparent time reference, the experience is that of *direct inspiration* or *illumination*. Such illumination is technically termed *seeing*, or, if it unfolds sluggishly due to insufficient energy or *personal power*, the experience is then of a *dreamlike* nature. Because very few apprentices have sufficient *personal power* to begin with, whenever the assemblage point shifts the experience thus gained is, technically speaking, termed *dreaming*.

During sleep man's assemblage point is no longer kept fixed by the First Attention and consequently it shifts around spontaneously, but chaotically – the results of which are what we generally experience as 'ordinary dreams'. Also, just as very few people have the necessary mental discipline to remember their ordinary dreams, so too do they mostly 'forget' left side experiences when the assemblage point returns to its normal position. To forget left side awareness in no way negates the influence of this knowledge; it merely results in this knowledge manifesting in a way which psychologists have termed *subconscious*, or *subliminal.* Even our ordinary dreams have a subconscious effect on our awareness, and thus also on our experience of life, as any depth psychologist will confirm.

Although this may come as a shock, average man generally *does not think*, because firstly, he never remembers his left side awareness, and secondly, he is incapable of effecting different permutations of perception within normal awareness. As a result, average man rarely comes up with original solutions to a specific problem, but instead tries his utmost to manipulate ideas and thoughts which he has inherited from his social upbringing to fit the problem at hand. This always results in what is termed *circling thought* or *internal dialogue,* and this in turn ultimately results in the man having to force a square peg into a round hole!

Those people who are capable of effecting some movement of the assemblage point, whether within the confines of the First Attention or into the Second Attention, are the real thinkers of the world. What man normally describes as a brainstorm or a flash of brilliance is inevitably the result of the assemblage point having moved. In this respect, it is worth noting how many so-called brilliant ideas were first perceived in dreams, regardless of whether these were daydreams or dreams ordinarily experienced during sleep.

Needless to say, the first task facing every apprentice is to harness enough *personal power* with which to move his assemblage point. First the apprentice must *move* his assemblage point within the confines of normal awareness so as to achieve clarity of vision, then he must learn to *shift* his assemblage point into heightened awareness in order to achieve altered states of perception.

The paradox which emerges at this point, and which always causes confusion, is that it is only through *intent* that it is possible to harness sufficient *personal power* with which to move or shift the assemblage point. It must be kept in mind that it is *intent* which causes us to perceive, and that *personal power* is the product of perception. *Intent* is defined as *the one and only force present throughout the universe* – it is quite simply the *unwavering will* or *purpose* of the Eagle. *Intent* is present within all forms of life, organic as well as inorganic, and therefore obviously manifests in a kaleidoscopic display of variations and differentiations.

The true purpose of the human being is to learn how to unfold and direct the force of *intent*, which is held as firmly within the awareness of man as it is within the awareness of the Eagle Itself. *Intent*, therefore, is not a strange and alien force, but the rightful heritage of man. Every one of us is born with the ability to develop *intent* to its maximum potential.

Here, however, it becomes important to define the terms *human* and *man*. Toltecs define the human being as the social person upon the physical plane, that is, the *tonal*. The prefix 'hu' has its original etymology in the Egyptian language, in which it means 'tiger'. Therefore the term *human* means literally 'tiger man', or quite simply, 'animal man'. It should be understood though, that it is not the *human being* who incarnates, but rather the *awareness* of the *nagal*. This awareness, which in the majority of esoteric schools has been termed the *re-incarnating ego*, is termed the *dreamer* in the Toltec teachings. The term *man*, therefore, is defined as being the totality of *nagal*, *dreamer* and *tonal*.

The concept of the dreamer goes far beyond the scope of this first volume, but it is mentioned here, firstly, to avoid unnecessary gaps in the information presented, and secondly, to point out that the *tonal* is often called the *dreamed*. In other words, during physical incarnation, the dreamer dreams, not only the *tonal*, but also the destiny of that *tonal*. This is an important concept to understand, because it is the *will* of man's dreamer to manifest *intent* through its instrument, the *tonal*, upon the physical plane. Therefore we can see that it is not so very difficult to cultivate *intent*, for it is inherent within every man's destiny to do so. All that is required is the necessary effort, and therein lies the value of the practical work.

One final topic must be covered in order to complete this section of the teachings. This topic concerns what is termed the Third Attention. Although, as has previously been explained, the Third Attention is generally not the direct concern of the majority of apprentices at this time, it does have some bearing on *intent* as well as on two other concepts which are today receiving world-wide interest, namely *meditation* and *magic*.

I have often been asked about the Toltec view on meditation. However, in order to understand the Toltec view it is important to have grasped the concept of the dreamer. Meditation is not circling thought, nor is it the random repeat of a mantra, because this boils down to internal dialogue. True meditation consists of complete inner silence – a silence in which there is only awareness. This awareness is of course the dreamer, and when that state is entered the social being is quite literally en rapport with his dreamer.

This in effect means that during meditation the practitioner enters into his full awareness, and in that state he is capable of understanding the purpose of his dreamer at that particular moment in time. It should therefore be clear that true meditation cannot take place before the practitioner has first mastered the art of silencing the internal dialogue. However, to stop the internal dialogue, like everything else, requires *personal power*.

In the end, it does not really matter what form of meditation is used, provided that it is practised in such a way that it leads to the silencing of the internal dialogue and the harnessing of *personal power*. This is the true purpose of all meditation techniques, but unfortunately most practitioners get caught up in either the form of the meditation, or else in the mantra, and consequently never reach the desired goal. For example, in Raja Yoga the man normally becomes obsessed with the act of visualization without realising that the visualization is merely an aid to stop the internal dialogue. Likewise, the man who uses a mantra meditation becomes obsessed with keeping the mantra going and does not realise that the mantra should at some point cease as inner silence takes over. In both of these examples it is the man's obsession which is his downfall and which keeps the assemblage point firmly fixed in normal awareness.

The important point here is that when the warrior has acquired sufficient *intent* he will be able to silence the internal dialogue, which will in turn enable him to break the fixation of his awareness and to make his assemblage point fluid. Once this has been accomplished the warrior not only enters the awareness of his dreamer, but he also becomes at-one with his dreamer, which is of course his *real self*. It is this state of being which is termed the Third Attention, a level of awareness in which the warrior can consciously manipulate his dreamer's expression of the one universal force, namely the *will of the Eagle*, or *intent*. Hence it is stated that there comes a time in the life of the warrior when the *command of the warrior becomes the command of the Eagle*.

This statement should not be confused with the religious concept of Unity of Consciousness or Universal Consciousness, or At-one-ment with God, or entering the Mind or Heart of God, or any other similar statements. In this respect, it must always be remembered that the Third Attention implies the ability to guide the assemblage point purposefully to any position within the Band of Man. Warriors are not so arrogant as to forget that by doing so they are merely moving within the confines of the *unknown*. This still leaves the *unknowable* untouched.

Man, being the microcosm of the macrocosm, does have the unknowable within him, but to access those energy fields is to venture beyond the Band of Man. This is perfectly possible, but to venture into the unknowable is to cease being human. There is no doubt that one day man will have reached a level of awareness which will enable him to enter safely the unthinkable vastness of the unknowable, but this is not the present purpose of the dreamers of mankind. Entering into the Third Attention is enough work and challenge for the majority of mankind at this time.

Taking all of the above into consideration, the Third Attention can be defined as *that* ***quality*** *of awareness which demonstrates itself as the* ***purpose*** *of the dreamer*. The effect of demonstrating this quality upon the physical plane is what average man calls magic, or a miracle. This purpose which we call magic is triple in nature and manifests as *movement, sound* and *colour*. Naturally this triplicity pertains to the dreamer. Upon the physical plane we find that *movement* corresponds to physical action, *sound* to thought and *colour* to emotion. Thus we say that *emotion initiates thought which materializes into action*.

It is not possible to say more about *intent* in this volume, except that magic by its truest possible definition is nothing more than the use of *intent* through the manipulation of colour, sound and movement, or emotion, thought and action. The only reason why this has been touched upon here is because it is vital to understand that emotion is the manifestation of the dreamer's *intent* upon the physical plane. Therefore, throughout all of the Toltec teachings it will be noticed that emotion is stressed again and again in one way or another.

In order to clear up any remaining confusion on the subject of magic it should be noted that magic has two possible manifestations. One of these forms, known as the *Second Ring of Power,* is that described above, in which the magician utilizes the power of *pure intent.* The other form is known as the *First Ring of Power*, an ancient form of magic based upon ritual, incantations, spells and formulas of every possible scope and description. This second form of magic, which is the most commonly-known form, is cumbersome and rather limited, as it is based on the *power* of the *tonal.*

It is a strange and deep mystery of the Toltec tradition, and as such generally not well understood, that the *tonal,* when perfectly controlled and disciplined, does have an inherent *power* of its own. This *power*, however, is not only limited in comparison to the power of *intent,* but is also exhaustible. A practitioner of this second kind of magic can therefore deplete himself and his *power*, something about which true Toltecs are not overly enthusiastic. Not only is *intent* far more practical and powerful, but it is also unlimited and inexhaustible. These two paths have also been termed respectively; The Greater and The Lesser Paths of Magic, The Major and Minor Powers, The Magician of Pure Intent and the Formula Magician, The Magician and The Shaman, etcetera.

It is important to remember that in the final analysis there is nothing except *intent* – the *will of the Eagle* – and that this *intent* manifests within man, firstly, as the colour of his dreamer, and secondly, as the emotion of his tonal. Therefore, in all of the practical work the task of the apprentice is to learn how to cultivate his natural heritage, *intent.* Once he has understood this the road lies clear ahead. One thing will lead to another until finally the apprentice acquires the knack of manipulating *intent,* which in turn leads him into being able to work also with sound and movement.

This implies that the apprentice then automatically becomes a magician, but this does not necessarily happen in the accepted sense of the word. There is far more to the magic of life than merely the phenomenal acts which engender so much awe. The true purpose of man's magical powers is not to entertain others, but to create in the true sense of the word. Sometimes, for one reason or another, it is important for a magician to be able to demonstrate his powers upon the physical plane, and when this is the case, then provided he puts in the needed time and effort, he will unfold this ability. However, it is not the fate of everyone within this particular lifetime to demonstrate these phenomenal powers.

The magician of *pure intent* is not a circus animal; his work requires the discipline and integrity of one who has understood the interrelationship of all life. Accordingly, the true magician involves himself with the intelligent co-operation between man and the forces of destiny, and he learns to utilize his magical powers in the eternal and magnificent play of creation. Such acts, however, happen behind the scenes, within worlds as yet not seen by mortal eyes. It is within these unseen worlds that all true Toltecs move, and it is there where they all commence the so-called *definitive journey of power*.

The key to the unseen worlds lies in the warrior's ability and expertise in handling first, *emotion*, and later, *intent*. Therefore the first practical task assigned to every apprentice is learning to recognize his emotions for what they truly are, and then learning to use them wisely.

At this point every apprentice will ask how he is supposed to use his emotions, and yet this question, inevitable as it may be, is totally invalid. The apprentice might just as well ask how he is supposed to use his lungs to breathe, or his legs to stand or walk! Such questions make no sense at all, for the simple reason that if you don't breathe you will die, and if you do not stand up on your legs you will not stay upright, let alone walk. Yet realise that none of us have ever been taught how to breathe or how to use our legs. Both these acts are simply acts of *intent* just like everything else we do, and in this respect using our emotions is not in any way different.

However, just as most people never learn to breathe deeply and fully, so the majority of people never learn to centre their body weight correctly so as to achieve maximum use of their body's muscular system. Any opera singer will confirm that to breathe properly is a specialised art, and any gymnast will admit that long before he or she can perform gymnastic feats many hours are spent over many years learning how to centre the body weight correctly and how to isolate and control the action of every muscle. The apprentice to the Warrior's Path undergoes a very similar training programme in learning the correct use of emotions. The point which is being stressed here is that we all breathe, we all use our bodies and we all use our emotions. Some of us just do it better than others.

There are very few people in the world who can really claim to be in control of their emotions. Most of the time, man's emotions are partially or totally suppressed, or else more or less out of his conscious control. Nevertheless, learning to unblock and to use emotions is not at all difficult, but it does require some careful consideration if unpleasant situations and unwanted circumstances are to be avoided. However, before we look at how to do this, it is important to clarify a point which all too often causes confusion.

The point in question concerns the difference between *feelings* and *emotions.* Realise that these two words are not identical or synonymous. Feelings can often spark off emotions, and for that matter so too can thoughts, but feelings are not emotions. The true nature of feeling will be dealt with in later volumes, but let it suffice for now to say that feelings are the *registering of left side knowledge* for which the rational mind has no frame of reference. Emotions, on the other hand, are secondary impulses generated by the act of perception, and depending on the individual's level of sobriety, will be either pure in their simplicity or else impure in their complexity.

In order to understand this it is necessry to know that there are only four pure emotions; namely, anger, fear, joy and melancholy. All other emotions are mixtures of two or more of these primary emotions, and as such are not pure. All four pure emotions are expressions of *desire*, the physical manifestation of the one universal force, *intent*. Anger is the *desire to fight*, fear is the *desire to retreat*, joy is the *desire to live* and melancholy is the *desire to change*.

From the above it should be clear why it is important for an apprentice to learn to recognise his emotions for what they truly are, for only in this way will he be able to use them wisely and to his advantage. The only way of doing this is to cultivate that level of awareness which is referred to as being *wide awake* – the very first prerequisite for walking the Warrior's Path. It is simply not possible to learn to become a warrior when one is half asleep. The warrior is fully conscious of which emotions are generated by the act of perception, what their cause is, as well as their purpose and also their potential.

In order to make it clear how emotions should be utilized, let us look at a few examples. Consider a man named Leon, who has a violent temper which is easily aroused. We have already seen earlier in this book the futility of suppressing emotions, but clearly Leon cannot allow his aggression to get out of control. If Leon is to succeed in becoming a warrior he must learn to handle his aggression skillfully, and also learn to use it as a tool in the technique of recapitulation.

In considering Leon's task, let us imagine that one day he sees his neighbour tossing some rubbish over the wall into his garden. Needless to say, Leon is instantly furious, but it will not help him simply to punch his neighbour on the nose. Although at that precise moment Leon would dearly love to rough up his neighbour, he knows he must not do so. At the same time, he cannot just ignore the incident. So Leon devises a plan of action. Taking a bag, he carefully sweeps up the rubbish and places it in the bag. Then he walks over to his neighbour's house and rings the doorbell.

Leon is still shaking with anger when his neighbour answers the door but, forcing himself to be calm, he politely hands his neighbour the bag of rubbish, saying: 'I believe you lost this in my garden.'

Red in the face with embarrassment, Leon's neighbour meekly takes the proffered bag and mumbles an apology. Leon merely grins, and after assuring his neighbour that it was his pleasure to have been able to return the lost goods, he turns from the door and leaves.

In this particular case Leon did not suppress his anger, but still acted impeccably whilst allowing his anger to fuel his actions. In the end Leon quite enjoyed himself, and learned that it is really quite good fun using emotions in this way. Furthermore, Leon also realised that in controlling his anger he had avoided what could have turned out to be a very unpleasant situation.

Had Leon not been aggressive, but timid instead, he could still have handled the situation in exactly the same way – this time allowing his anger to fuel his courage. Alternatively, if he did not deem it wise to confront his neighbour directly, he could simply have placed the bag in front of his neighbour's door, together with a polite note requesting the neighbour kindly to refrain from this sort of behaviour in the future. The effect would have been the same, and either way Leon would have accomplished his task.

Let us now consider a woman named Lydia, who is normally very shy and easily offended. In fact, unlike Leon, Lydia is not at all aggressive, but has spent most of her life in fear of what people can say or do to her. Then one day her sister comes to visit and, without meaning to offend, she teases Lydia about her weight. Immediately Lydia feels offended and self-conscious about her figure but, instead of keeping quiet as she would normally have done, Lydia reacts in a manner which takes her sister by surprise.

Thinking quickly, Lydia places her hands squarely on her hips, and feigning an indignation which she does not feel, boldly addresses her sister:'I welcome your visit here, sister dear,' Lydia retorts tersely, 'and even if I am fat at least I have the decency to make my sister feel at home.'

Caught off-guard by Lydia's unexpected reaction, the sister hurriedly tries to make amends for her thoughtless teasing, but again Lydia throws her sister off balance by laughing heartily and waving aside her sister's apology. Uncertain now of how to proceed further, Lydia's sister carefully refrains from making personal remarks about Lydia for the rest of the visit.

Lydia has won the battle, simply because she refused to react in her accustomed manner when slighted, and therefore instead of giving in to her fear Lydia used her fear to spark off her wit. In other words, although in the past Lydia would have withdrawn into herself because of her fear that perhaps her body was not as trim as it could be, this time she allowed her fear of further teasing to help her fight back. In that moment of spontaneous retaliation the first weapon that came to hand was Lydia's sense of wit, and with it she turned the tables on her sister.

In another example we see that a man called William is suffering from what he believes to be depression because his wife has filed for divorce. However, on a closer look William realises that his so-called depression is merely a secondary effect of a deep sense of melancholy. Furthermore, in thinking about it, he begins to see that his melancholy has followed a definite pattern throughout his life, and apparently always surfaces just prior to his having to face some major change in his circumstances.

Having come to this realisation, William now has two choices open to him; firstly, he can try and suppress his sadness, or secondly, he can flow with it to see what gift of *power* it holds for him. Obviously, it is no easy task for William just to walk away from a woman he has loved and lived with for over ten years, yet he also knows that she would not have filed for divorce if she had really wanted the marriage to last.

Deciding not to suppress his sadness, William allows himself to experience its full impact, and much to his surprise finds that the sadness has swept away all his feelings of being wronged by his wife. In that moment of clarity it is suddenly very clear to William that it is not he his wife wants to divorce, but rather that she is desperate to get away from the behaviour patterns he has developed since their marriage began. Remembering now that his wife has been complaining for some time that he is no longer the man she married, it is suddenly very clear to William that a divorce will change nothing. Instead what is required is that he should change the behaviour patterns which are causing the rift in his marriage. Feeling suddenly elated rather than depressed, William decides to fight for his marriage.

A young woman, Cynthia, is on her way to a job interview but is terribly nervous and keeps worrying that she might not get the job. Knowing that her worry is only making her more nervous, Cynthia decides to try and think about something else, and so she imagines how happy she will be if she does get the job. For a few brief moments Cynthia experiences a very real feeling of joy, and although the feeling is fleeting, it is nevertheless enough to make her realise that she can go to the interview tense and worried or relaxed and happy. Knowing full well that all the worry in the world is not going to change anything, Cynthia once again directs her focus onto happier thoughts, and consequently by the time she is sitting in front of her prospective employer she has brought her nervousness under control and is able to conduct herself in an easy and cheerful way throughout the interview. In other words, Cynthia has used joy to bring her nervousness and worry under control.

From the examples we have looked at it should now be clear

how an apprentice is expected to go about, first, getting to know his emotions, and second, learning to use them to his advantage. Realise, however, that although it is not at all difficult to use emotions, it is altogether a different ball-game to use them consciously and efficiently. To use emotions to one's advantage is a specialised skill which can only be acquired through constant practice and in conjunction with the technique of not-doing, a technique which will be dealt with later on. The reader is therefore urged to study not-doing in the light of what has been said here in relation to working with emotion. This in turn will ultimately lead to a deeper understanding of that elusive force termed *intent*, a concept which transcends the scope of this volume, but to which we will return again and again in volumes to come. Furthermore, using emotions is also a vital prerequisite in the technique of recapitulation, and in the following chapter we will look at how this is to be tackled.

THE DREAMER OF MANKIND

'All that we see or seem
Is but a dream within a dream.'
Edgar Allan Poe

(Pencil drawing: Susan Emily)

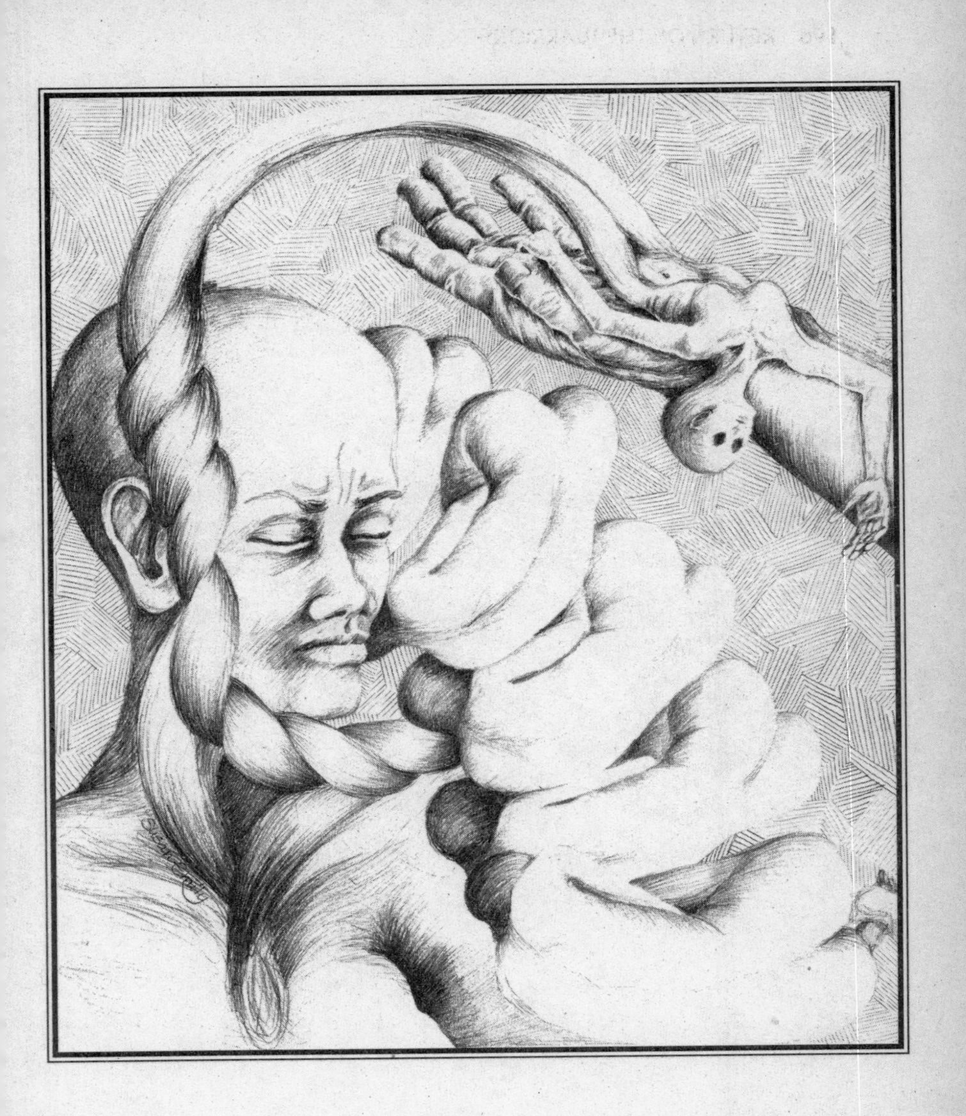

CHAPTER EIGHT

RECAPITULATION

In order to understand the technique of recapitulation it is vital to grasp clearly the true nature of man's luminous cocoon. This cocoon, which contains the life force, is really an electromagnetic* force field composed of an incalculable number of energy filaments. These filaments are not singular strands of energy, but are made up of minute energy fibres. In other words, energy fibres are correlated electromagnetic impulses existing within a unified spectrum termed an energy field. Furthermore, awareness is also electromagnetic in nature,

---

**Toltecs view the entire universe as being a manifestation of electrical phenomena which is essentially triple in nature. This tripilicity is tabulated as follows:*

Tonal	*Movement*	*Activity*	*Electrical Manifestation of matter*
Dreamer	*Colour*	*Magnetism*	*Electrical Manifestation of awareness*
Nagal	*Sound*	*Vitality*	*Electrical Manifestation of the life-force*

Scientists as yet only recognise the electrical manifestation of matter and will only discover and understand the other two forms once they turn their attention to the study of man as a non-corporeal being.

and what is termed the assemblage point is in fact the inherent awareness of the life-force. Therefore, whenever the assemblage point illumines a group of energy fields, it implies that awareness is vibrating at a frequency which is compatible with that of the fields on which it is centred.

These energy fibres arise as a result of the movement or interaction between atoms. Another way of expressing this is to define an energy fibre as the electromagnetic interrelationship between two atoms. It is therefore obvious to see that such fibres are extremely delicate and fragile, and that it does not take much effort to 'damage' them in such a way that they become displaced. Normally it will only be some fibres within a field which become displaced, while the overall field will appear unaffected. But when enough fibres have become displaced the field itself becomes 'damaged'.

In man's daily life he is constantly interacting emotionally with the world around him. This interaction is only possible because of perception; that is, perception accounts for the emotional responses to any given situation. These emotions spark off certain thoughts, and it is the interrelationship between the emotional responses and thoughts which determines the action man will take.

Emotional responses are caused by the electromagnetic impulses generated by the act of perception. It must be remembered that when a man aligns his energy fields with those outside his cocoon perception takes place. This in effect means that the awareness of the observer sets up primary electromagnetic impulses, which are then transferred to the observed via the energy fields by means of the electromagnetic impulses constituting the fields. This is somewhat similar to the manner in which electricity is conducted by the movement of electrons. Obviously the observed will perceive the observer simultaneously in the same fashion. When the impulses initiated by both the observer and observed meet, they mingle and interact to set up secondary impulses. These secondary impulses, relayed back to both observer and observed via the energy fields, are what man interprets as emotion.

Normally, the process involved in perception causes no harm at all, but should the emotional responses generated be sufficiently powerful or violent, some of the fibres within the energy fields can become displaced. In other words, either the observer loses some of his fibres to the observed, or vice versa, or they can both inherit some of the other's fibres. Exactly how this displacement takes place is too complex to explain here. Suffice it to say that emotion can cause a person's energy fields to become permanently changed, either by becoming depleted of some of their former strength, or by becoming polluted through the addition of extraneous force.

Since the average man has a fixed assemblage point he confines himself to using only one group of energy fields. It therefore stands to reason that in the course of time the energy fields he uses become increasingly 'threadbare' and polluted. This is the technical explanation of the effects of social conditioning, and as this deterioration continues, so perception itself becomes increasingly impure and inaccurate. Thus the task of the apprentice is to 'purify' his energy fields, firstly, by expelling all foreign fibres from within his cocoon, and secondly, by reclaiming those fibres he has lost.

Although all this appears to be very obscure and mystical, orthodox science itself is not that far away from understanding the unity of life. Life is essentially a web of interrelated, interactive and interdependant electromagnetic forces, and whatever happens to even the minutest component of the web has an effect upon the entire web. Within this matrix of force there is a continuous flow of motion as energy is transferred along and across the electromagnetic currents forming the web. It is not the purpose of this book to explain man's relationship to the universe, but at least some explanation is needed in order to grasp the concept of energy transference or displacement.

The best that can be done in this book is to give an

extremely simplified description of this process. Losing fibres or reclaiming fibres is not so much a case of dealing with personal particles, but rather a case of what is termed *adjustment*. In other words, when a warrior reclaims fibres lost to another person, he does not literally retrieve those lost fibres from the person concerned, but merely takes the needed fibres from the web. This action naturally throws the web out of balance, and in order to restore its own balance the web in turn reclaims these fibres from the person who took them from the warrior. The same applies even if the warrior has to reclaim fibres from a deceased person, because these fibres are pure energy and as such are not bound by time and space. Likewise, when a warrior expels foreign fibres he simply rejects them into the web, and the web will in turn restore them to where they really belong.

In order to accomplish this the apprentice must recapitulate every experience he has ever had, right down to the last detail. When first confronted with this apparently herculean task every apprentice feels completely overwhelmed, yet it is not really as impossible as it appears. So that man may achieve the maximum evolution of awareness from any given experience, the life force has a habit of repeating experiences in clearly defined cycles, and anyone who is sufficiently interested can quite easily trace these cycles in his own life. Thus the majority of experiences in a man's life are merely 'repeat performances'.

In view of this, recapitulation boils down to having to recapitulate fully only one cycle in our lives. The other cycles will then be found to be merely repetitions and will therefore be rapidly assimilated. This is not to imply that recapitulation is easy or quick, but simply that it is not an insurmountable task. A full recapitulation, right up to the moment of birth, is vital, and it normally takes many years of constant and diligent labour. However, it is not necessary for an apprentice to have a total recall of his life before he can progress upon the Warrior's Path – every bit of recapitulation completed aids him in moving forward, and every movement has a snowball effect in that it gathers momentum and power.

In relation to the practical work it is an excellent practice to keep a journal of the work done and the knowledge gained. Such a journal helps greatly in cultivating discipline and an ordered approach to the teachings. Eventually, once a certain threshold of understanding has been crossed, journals are no longer needed, in which case they will normally end up on a bookshelf somewhere as personal memoirs; but until such time, they serve an invaluable purpose. After all, the Warrior's Path is the most important and exhilarating journey for anyone to undertake; it is the journey of all journeys, and all worthwhile journeys should be recorded in a journal.

In working with a journal everything to do with the Warrior's Path should be entered in one book, rather than having different journals for different aspects of the work. This may at first appear to be somewhat chaotic, but it does have the advantage of highlighting undercurrents and details which can easily be overlooked when working from several different books. Therefore, note everything in one journal – recapitulation, experiences, dreams, notes, thoughts, etcetera. When the journal is full, start a new one. You should discipline yourself to make at least one entry in the journal every day. Another good habit is to date these entries for future cross-reference.

Recapitulation is usually abbreviated to 'recapping' by most apprentices and consists of two types, namely, *active recapitulation* and spontaneous or *passive recapitulation*. In active recapping, the apprentice sits down and formally recalls incidents from his past, whereas in spontaneous recapping an incident experienced in the moment sparks off the memory of an experience from the past. For optimum use of time apprentices are expected to avail themselves of both types of recapping. In practice it will normally be found that spontaneous recapping yields the most beneficial results to begin with. On the other hand, active recapping is often initially slow and laborious, but as such is invaluable for exercising the *intent*. Once the *intent* is sufficiently strong, recapping is equally facilitated by both methods.

At the outset all apprentices unwittingly fall into the trap of recalling intellectual memories of the past. It must be stressed that this is not recapping, but merely what Toltecs call 'bookkeeping'. Such intellectual memories should be used only as guides to recapping. Real recapping means having to relive an incident as if it is happening in the moment. This entails the necessity of having to recall and re-experience every single emotion that was generated by that incident. Only by recalling those emotions can we relive an incident fully and decipher what actually took place. Likewise, it is only once we know what really happened that we are in a position to expel foreign fibres and to reclaim the fibres of our own which may have been lost in the experience.

ACTIVE RECAPITULATION

In order to set up recapping it does not matter where we begin, because in any event we ultimately need an entire recall. Obviously the most logical place to start is with the most significant events from one's recent past. It is a good idea for the apprentice to make a list of all the major incidents he or she can remember, starting from the recent past and working backwards in time. This is what is known as setting up active recapping. Once the apprentice has made his list he simply takes the first incident on the list and recalls as much detail as he can. There must be no sense of hurrying because the more detail he can remember the easier it will be to uncover the emotions he experienced at the time. In applying this the apprentice will find an old adage most useful – '*make haste slowly.*'

An apprentice working under the guidance of a nagal will sometimes be given a breathing exercise to accompany his recapping, but such exercises can be dangerous if not properly monitored and are, strictly speaking, not essential to the actual technique of recapping. The breathing can be a help, but recapping can be just as successful and a lot safer without it. In this book breathing exercises are therefore deliberately omitted for the sake of safety.

The best way to understand the technique of recapping is by working through an example. An apprentice working under the guidance of a nagal will, with that teacher's assistance, work through an actual experience in his life, but for the purposes of this book we will have to settle for a hypothetical example. Let us consider a man named Peter, who constantly feels guilty because he believes he is a coward.

In Peter's recent past he had an experience in which he felt he should have spoken up for his rights, but instead of doing so he kept quiet and allowed the situation to pass. Thinking back on his life, Peter can see that this is an old habit of his, especially when he senses that if he speaks up he might find himself being confronted physically. Remembering when he was at school, Peter realises that he avoided all forms of physical confrontation and violence, even to the point of hating contact sport. As a child, Peter had often been tormented by being called a coward and had grown up believing this was true.

Yet in reflecting on his life as a whole, Peter realises that there have been many instances when he did not behave like a coward, but on the contrary acted with more courage than most people would have managed. Herein Peter finds his first clue, namely that he only behaves like a coward when he senses physical violence. At first this baffles Peter, for he knows that he is no weakling, and although he is not a big man, he is nevertheless extremely strong for his size.

Reflecting deeper on his problem, Peter remembers that whenever he was taunted as a child he would seethe with anger, but also shake with the fear of being physically hurt. Peter's fear of being hurt always caused him to run away from a fight, and then afterwards he would despise himself for having done so. This had been the pattern of Peter's childhood, and in thinking back, Peter could not remember a time when this was not the case.

In trying to recap, Peter suddenly recalls an incident which took place a few years before. In that incident he was working in his garage when suddenly a stray cat who was being chased by a neighbour's dog came running into the garage to dive into the open drawer of a cupboard. After the dog had gone Peter at first tried to get the cat out of the drawer, but the cat refused to come out. Although Peter has always been an animal lover, the cat's refusal to come out somehow infuriated him. Without even thinking, he started to yell and swear at the cat, but when even this did not dislodge the animal, he became beside himself with anger.

Feeling furious, Peter grabbed an old rolled-up newspaper, and setting this alight, thrust it into the drawer in an attempt to scare the cat out of its hiding place. However, the cat still did not budge, and so, after stamping out the flames of the newspaper, Peter yanked the drawer completely out of the cupboard in a fit of rage. Cowering in the corner of the drawer was the cat, wide-eyed with fear, and his whiskers all singed from the flames. Seeing the cat, Peter's anger dissipated in an instant, leaving him feeling aghast and ashamed at what he had done. He realised that the cat was not harmed, but was nevertheless thoroughly terrified. Staring into the eyes of the petrified animal, Peter experienced a jab of devastating regret and an overwhelming feeling of pity for the cat.

Peter's actions on that day haunted him for months afterwards. Every time he recalled the incident he cringed from the feelings of guilt and shame. Somehow this only confirmed to Peter what a coward he really was, since he would not stand up for his rights with people, but would instead take his anger out on a frightened and defenceless animal.

Still trying to recap, Peter one day remembers yet another incident, which took place at work sometime after the experience with the cat. On that particular morning Peter's boss laid down the law concerning employees who were late for work. At lunchtime, Peter went quickly to buy some paint he needed, but on his way back to work he was very badly delayed in the traffic and consequently arrived a few minutes late. As fate would have it, Peter's boss was waiting for him and as Peter came in through the door his boss almost lifted the roof with his anger.

At first Peter stood dead still, frozen to the spot, whilst his boss ranted and raved like a lunatic. Then suddenly a white-hot anger came over Peter, causing a strange ringing in his ears and leaving his hands trembling.

Peter's boss was standing with his back towards a full-length mirror during the confrontation, and for some reason Peter looked past his boss at the mirror. Seeing the back of his boss reflected in the mirror an angry thought flashed through Peter's mind. In that instant Peter decided to put his boss in his place, and as the thought took shape Peter could feel the surge of adrenalin in his body. Angered beyond speech, he was ready for murder, and wanted nothing more than to smash the mirror with his boss's head. In his blind fury he could already see the mirror shatter, its jagged splinters smeared with the blood of his boss.

Fortunately for Peter, a colleague standing to his side must have sensed his blind fury, for he suddenly reached out to put a restraining hand on Peter's shoulder. The colleague's touch somehow had the effect of bringing Peter back to a sense of sobriety, thereby dispelling most of his anger. In the end Peter merely glared angrily at his boss before walking away quietly.

For days afterwards Peter puzzled over his reaction to his boss. His fury at having been shouted at and his consequent lust for revenge had been completely out of proportion, especially as Peter knew that he had been at fault in coming late for work. Although Peter could not put his finger on it he somehow knew that this incident, like the one with the cat, had something to do with his attempts at trying to recap.

Then one day Peter suddenly recalls an incident which occurred between him and one of his cousins when they were both about five years old. The two of them were playing under a tree where Peter had built himself a little hut out of twigs and sticks. When the hut was finished Peter was just on the point of crawling inside when his cousin pushed his way into the hut ahead of him. Since the hut was too small to accommodate both boys simultaneously, Peter tried to persuade his cousin to come out so that he could have a turn at being in the hut. Peter's cousin, however, was in a teasing mood and would not relent. Suddenly Peter became furious, and grabbing his cousin by the arm, tried to pull him out. Peter pulled with all his might, becoming more and more aggressive, but when he realised that his cousin was not going to budge, he bit the boy's arm with a vengeance.

Needless to say, Peter's cousin fled out of the hut screaming and wailing at the top of his voice. This was the first time that Peter had ever been compelled to stand up for his rights, and also the first time he had ever been involved in a physical confrontation. Nevertheless, Peter was horrified by his cousin's reaction, and in that moment realised what he had done. Not knowing what else to do, Peter meekly crawled into his little hut, feeling confused, uncertain, and somehow very guilty and sordid.

Within minutes Peter's mother arrived on the scene to find out what all the commotion was about. When she saw the mark Peter's teeth had left on his cousin's arm, she reached into the hut and, grabbing Peter by the arm, hauled him out. By this time Peter knew he had done something very wrong. To crown it all he also realised that he had, through his actions, angered his mother. Up until that fateful moment he had always been able to turn to his mother when he felt insecure and uncertain, but now he had no–one to turn to.

Right in front of his cousin, Peter's mother gave him the beating of his life. In recalling the incident, Peter can clearly remember every detail of that episode, and he relives the entire ordeal with every feeling flooding back. He experiences again the shock, the fright and the pain of being beaten, the horror of what he had done, and above all, the emotional pain caused by his mother's anger. The overall experience of that moment left Peter with a feeling of deep shame and confusion.

Continuing to recap, Peter now realises that from that day onwards he had avoided confrontations, but still had not been able to shake off the feeling of having betrayed his mother's love for him. Peter continued to feel inexorably ashamed and hated himself for what he had done. He remembers that during the years after that fateful day he often caught glimpses of his violent temper, but came to fear it more than anything else in his life as a defect which caused him to betray the one thing he needed so much – his mother's trust. This was the beginning of a lifetime's suppression of his aggression, in which fearing the consequences of allowing that aggression to surface, Peter chose instead to become timid. This of course caused him to suffer endless teasing and taunting, but in his child's mind this was justifiable retribution for having betrayed his mother's love.

Peter has punished himself for most of his life, and it was only when he recapped this incident that he finally understood his apparent cowardice. Realising at last what really took place on that day with his cousin, Peter is now in a position to rectify the situation. However, the work which now has to follow should also not be hurried, because any incident has more than just one effect upon our lives. Through the interrelationship of life, even an apparently insignificant incident will send forth ripple effects which permeate every aspect of our lives.

Before we look at how Peter should rectify what happened to him, let us first look at how the recapping could have come about through the process of spontaneous recapitulation.

SPONTANEOUS RECAPITULATION

We already know of Peter's problem, but Peter has a mental block in trying to recall what could possibly have triggered off his feelings of being a coward. This is not uncommon in recapping, especially when the original incident has been traumatic enough. A child, especially, will often block out the memory of a traumatic experience by spontaneously moving the assemblage point after the incident. When this happens the child will afterwards not be able to remember the incident readily, and the memory will become even more difficult to access later on in adulthood.

Peter has already relived the experiences with both the cat and his boss, but still he cannot recall what brought about his apparent cowardice. Then one day he visits some friends who have two small boys. While sitting with his friends on the patio overlooking their garden where the boys are playing some game or other, Peter looks up just in time to see one little boy bite his brother fiercely on the arm. As the injured boy lets out a piercing scream, Peter's memory is jolted, and in that instant he remembers most clearly and graphically every detail of that day when he bit his cousin.

This is an example of the typical way in which spontaneous

recapitulation usually takes place. However, it does not always require having to witness a scene. At times, simply being told about someone else's experience is sufficient to trigger the memory. At other times, one word will suffice. Sometimes the person concerned may first have to go through an almost identical scenario before being able to remember. The fact remains, though, that one way or another we can always revive our memories, for none of us ever really forget anything at all. Apparent loss of memory is always due either to a mental block, or to a slight movement of the assemblage point. By using the technique of recapping we can, if we wish, recall every detail of our lives.

Now that Peter has remembered the incident with his cousin, let us look at what he should do next. The first thing Peter should do is to recognise all the many effects which that incident has had upon his life as a whole. In this respect we will look at only a few examples, but in practice it is essential that every effect should be found and dealt with. Here again, it is a good idea to make a list.

In making his list of effects, Peter realises just how deeply he was scarred on that day with his cousin. Firstly, there had been the anger and frustration, followed by the shock at realising he had done something bad. This had been compounded by his mother's reaction, her displeasure and her anger at Peter, which ended in his being beaten. Finally there had been Peter's confusion, and his sense of shame and guilt, but, above all, the deep nagging feeling of having betrayed his mother's trust in him.

On that day, Peter lost many of the fibres that gave him confidence in fighting his own battles, and in their place he inherited from his mother those fibres which etched deeply upon his mind the knowledge that it is a bad thing to fight. With this, he also lost many of the fibres that gave him the confidence to express his anger, and because of his love for his mother, he had drawn from her fibres of timidity in an attempt to compensate for his wrong actions.

Before that fateful day Peter had never known what it was to be ashamed, but because of his cousin's reaction, Peter inherited from him fibres which gave him a deep sense of shame. Furthermore, because of his mother's reaction, Peter also inherited from her fibres which sparked off in him a sense of guilt at what he had done.

In the midst of all the ensuing commotion, Peter lost to both his mother and his cousin some of the fibres that enabled him to distinguish between right and wrong. In his confusion, Peter totally forgot that he had been wronged by his cousin in the first place, and consequently inherited from him fibres which made Peter blame himself for wrongs that someone else committed against him. Peter also took from his mother fibres which made him feel utterly ashamed at having betrayed her love for him. For the first time in his young life, Peter had come to know the meaning of being a traitor, and so, in his love for his mother, he tried to compensate by wresting from her fibres which brought about a destructive demand for self-punishment.

This gives some idea of the exchange of fibres that took place on that day and how the effects scarred Peter for most of his life. One of the worst things was Peter's unconscious decision to suppress his aggression from then onwards. The ill-effects brought about by such suppression have already been dealt with earlier in this book, but for Peter it also had several secondary effects.

The major secondary effect was Peter's feeling of being a coward. As a result of constantly being teased about being a coward and a sissy, he gradually began to avoid all confrontations, including the teasing, until eventually he himself believed in his cowardice. Miserable and frightened of confrontation, even of teasing, Peter became shy, introverted and very much a loner. Totally lacking in self-confidence, Peter became even more insecure with people until finally he could feel secure only when he was left alone to play or work quietly by himself.

After recapping this incident, Peter now realises what really took place in the experiences he had with the cat and with his boss. On both occasions he had come close to recalling the incident with his cousin. The way the cat dashed into the garage, hid in the drawer and then refused to come out had stirred Peter's memory of when his cousin invaded his hut. Likwise, when Peter's boss shouted at him for coming late to work he had momentarily experienced a violent anger at being intimidated, for in that moment years of pent-up aggression suddenly surfaced and Peter saw his boss as a symbol of all the teasing and taunting he endured as a child.

Now that Peter knows where his feelings of cowardliness originated he can see that in reality he has never ever been a coward. On the contrary, it had taken all of his courage to endure the endless taunting, and every ounce of his control not to give in to his suppressed aggression. Once such a realisation has taken place the whole process has already begun to be reversed. The only thing left for Peter to do is systematically to reject the foreign fibres in his cocoon, and to reclaim the ones he has lost. This he will do through the technique of not-doing.

CONTROLLED FOLLY

What controls your folly - your own destiny, or social conditioning?
(Pencil drawing: Susan Emily)

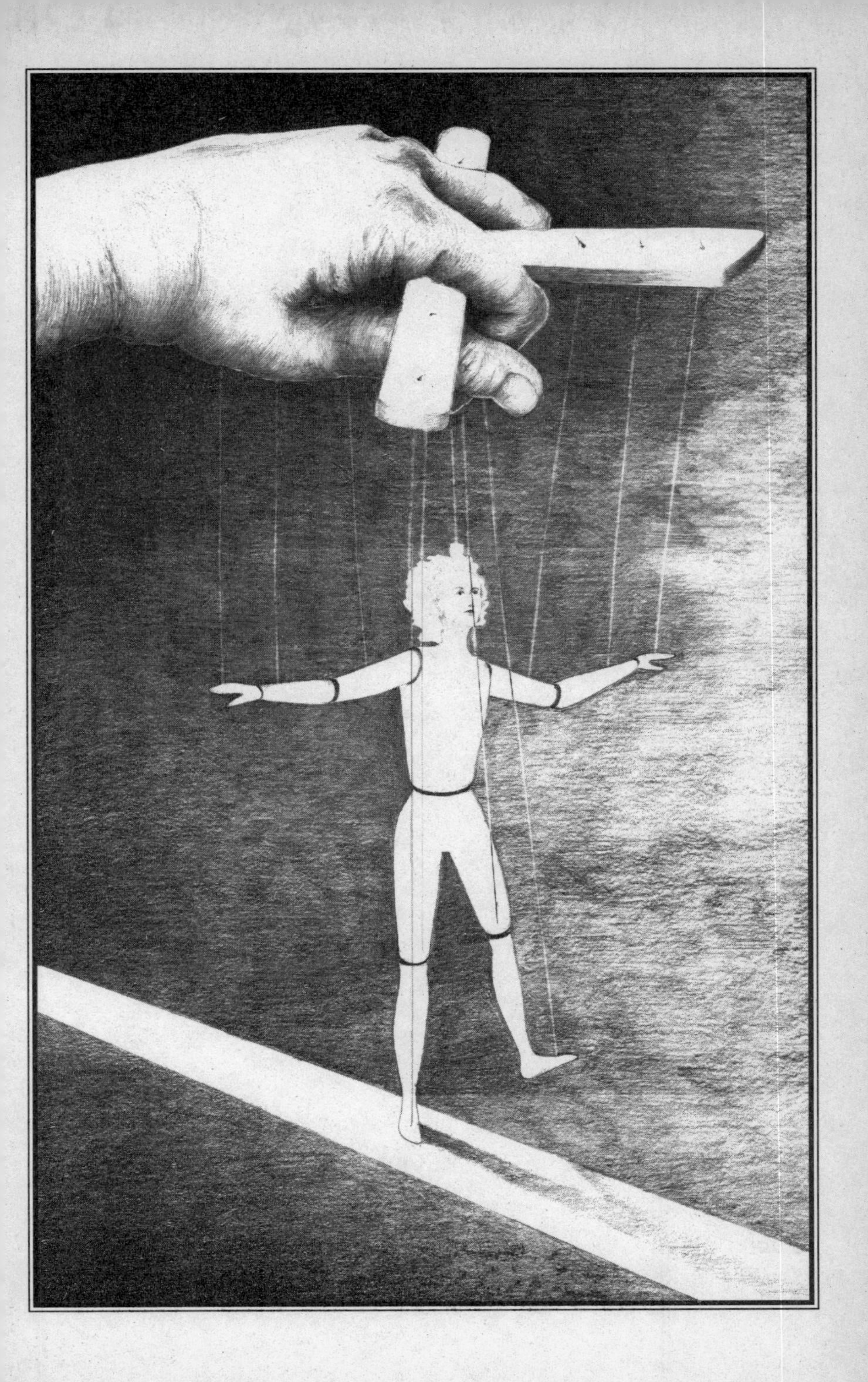

CHAPTER NINE

NOT-DOING AND STALKING

The technique of not-doing is in fact identical to stalking, because not-doing is the art of stalking oneself as opposed to stalking someone else. Both techniques are defined as *a calculated act designed to manipulate.* In learning to break free from the restraints of social conditioning, an apprentice must learn to stalk both himself and those around him. In this respect, stalking others may at first sight be viewed as immoral, but if the truth be told, every man, woman and child learns very quickly to manipulate the world around them, and continues to do so throughout their lives. The fact that everybody engages in manipulation does of course not justify it, but if one looks at stalking carefully the differences between stalking and common manipulation become obvious.

Manipulation as is commonly practised can never be condoned no matter who participates in it. When a man manipulates another to do his bidding or to agree with his point of view, the man is quite literally forcing his will upon his victim. Forcing one's will upon another being, for whatever reason, is an act of black magic and boils down to rape, whether physical, emotional or mental. People rape those around them constantly, and in their ignorance they actually take pride in their acts. Two different examples might help to make this point clearer.

Consider a man who has an employee by the name of John. John is still young and very enthusiastic about his job. Seeing John's enthusiasm, his employer constantly assures John that if he continues to work hard he can expect a bright future with the company. In his enthusiasm John works harder and harder, and spends more and more time at work. Very soon he is doing twice as much work as his job actually warrants, but in his eagerness he does not mind at all.

It is not long before John receives a raise in salary as well as a promotion. Thrilled by the results of his efforts, he now works even harder, and after yet another raise in salary he is ecstatically happy. However, he now spends even more time, including weekends, at work. As a result John no longer has the time to spend with friends, or just to relax at home. In fact, he has no spare time at all and can no longer do anything other than think about work.

Admittedly, John is happy and so too is his boss. Never before has his boss had such a diligent worker and, to John, his boss is the fairest and most appreciative employer he could ever have hoped for. On the surface everything seems quite honest and fair, and John continues to pour all of his energy and time into his work. Eventually he is promoted to the position of junior director, together with the appropriate salary, fringe benefits and a company car. In short, John is a made man.

However, underneath all this success lies a horrid truth. John's employer has exploited John's enthusiasm for his work until John's natural enthusiasm has become greed for success. In the end John has no life other than his work, and both his own and his boss's greed has turned him into nothing more than a money-making machine. He is no longer an enthusiastic and free-thinking young man, but just a man who is as firmly addicted to his work as another man may be to alcohol or drugs. John was enticed by promises of glory, and then mentally raped. In his ignorance he allowed it to happen, and he even feels gratitude towards his boss for what has taken place.

Let us also look at the case of a young lady named Janet, who has lived alone with her mother ever since her father died in an accident. Janet had always been a good scholar and daughter, working hard at school and helping her mother as much as possible in running their small home. After Janet completed her schooling she wanted to study dress design, but this did not meet with her mother's approval. Janet's mother was very firm on the issue, and spelt it out to Janet in no uncertain terms that the only reason she worked so hard after her husband's death was so that Janet could go to university to study something worthwhile.

Janet's mother wanted her to study medicine, and although Janet had no interest in becoming a doctor she did not want to disappoint her mother. Being a sensitive girl, she was always fully aware of how hard her mother had worked, especially after her father's death. Now her mother was using her sacrifice as a lever to play upon Janet's feelings of guilt. In the end, Janet relented and went to university, and in time qualified as a doctor.

Janet's mother has never hesitated to point out that it is thanks to her that Janet has succeeded in life and, in an attempt to show her gratitude for everything her mother has done, Janet buys a beautiful house for her mother to share with her. Janet is not happy in her work, but because of her nature she works hard as a doctor. Her mother, on the other hand, now has the chance to relax at home after a long life of hardship, and bask in her daughter's success. Social conditioning has made Janet believe that this is how it should be, but the sad truth is that she has been emotionally raped by her own mother and still allows the process to continue day in and day out.

In both of the examples above it is clear to see how people allow themselves to be manipulated and, because of social conditioning there are always those who are only too happy to oblige. However, this is not the kind of manipulation a true warrior will ever engage in. Such acts of psychological violence are abhorrent to the man who believes in freedom. Stalking is different to common manipulation in that stalking leads to freedom, whereas manipulation leads to slavery.

When a warrior stalks another being it is admittedly still manipulation, but it is nevertheless an act which is designed to bring about not only the warrior's freedom, but also the freedom of the being he is stalking. The examples of Leon and Lydia, used in Chapter Seven, were in fact examples both of stalking and not-doing. By not allowing themselves to react in their accustomed manner, but choosing instead a different but calculated course of action, Leon and Lydia were practising not-doing. Likewise, through their calculated actions they also taught their opponents something about the proper way in which to behave towards one's fellow creatures. In the end, both Leon and Lydia as well as their opponents benefited, which is the way it should be, for this is the basis of the interdependence of all life. However, as will be stressed again later in this chapter, a warrior never uses stalking to gain an unfair advantage, and he never takes it upon himself to teach people a lesson unless they have called one forth from him through their actions.

NOT-DOING

It is really quite easy to understand the concept of not-doing, but putting it into practice needs skill, and this can only be acquired through constant discipline. Basically, not-doing involves being fully alert all the time whilst observing one's emotional responses carefully. This constant vigilance inculcates in the practitioner a sense of *detachment* which gives him the necessary 'space' in order to be completely objective. It is a widely known fact that we can always see a situation much more clearly when we are objective observers than when we are involved in the situation ourselves. The practice of not-doing enables the warrior always to be an objective witness, even in situations in which he himself is deeply involved.

The warrior must not only be fully alert and objective, but he must also use the emotion he is experiencing in the moment to fuel his actions. This is important because, firstly, his actions will then be reflexive and quick, and secondly, his actions will have that spontaneity which lends vitality and impact. It is simply not possible to practise not-doing when one is half asleep.

Not-doing is the *act of playing a role chosen in the moment*, but since we never know what the next moment is going to bring, such acting necessitates the ability to *improvise*. In the beginning this is difficult for everyone, but as one develops an understanding of oneself, so one can begin to anticipate what one's emotional responses are going to be. Getting to know oneself is one of the reasons why the technique of recapitulation is so very important. Obviously, the better we know ourselves the more we can anticipate, and hence not-doing becomes easier and easier, quite apart from the fact that it is most enjoyable!

In not-doing we deliberately choose to enact a role which is diametrically opposed to our long-standing and habitual behaviour. If, therefore, an apprentice is usually lacking in confidence, he will practise not-doing by deliberately acting like a man who is fully confident. The apprentice is well aware of the fact that this is merely an act, but if he plays his part superbly those around him will become convinced that he really is very confident. Noting his spectators' reactions to his not-doing, the apprentice becomes encouraged to start believing in his ability to play his chosen role.

In the beginning this will change nothing, but if the apprentice repeatedly acts like a confident man he will slowly but surely continue to gain confidence in his ability to *enact* confidence. Once this process has been initiated the apprentice will continue to gain confidence in his chosen role until finally he begins to *live* his role. In living his role the apprentice will in time be overtaken by the role he is playing, and one day, without even realising when the transformation has taken place, the apprentice will realise that he has become confident in the true sense of the word. Whereas the apprentice had always lacked confidence in the past, he has now become the very epitome of confidence.

The games we play with ourselves, or with others, are very powerful because, although man is generally not aware of it, these games are games of *power* fuelled by *intent*. Any game we play starts off as a game, but if we play it well for long enough, it ends up as reality. Not-doing is a warrior's game; a game he plays with himself, a kind of psychological solitaire. This is what is known as *stalking oneself*. By playing not-doing the warrior can and does regain the fibres he has lost and can reject those which are foreign to his cocoon.

However, this is not the last of the benefits and effects of not-doing. By practising not-doing the warrior also knows that he is slowly but surely loosening his assemblage point and moving it fraction by fraction. An analogy might help to make this point clearer. If the assemblage point is like a rusty nut on the bolt of our old habits, then not-doing is like a deep-penetrating oil, and our motive for practising not-doing is like the spanner with which we are trying to undo the nut. What we call motive is nothing less than *intent*! In time, not-doing will saturate and soften the rust of social conditioning, and our constant attempt at trying to loosen the nut will strengthen the *intent* until it is strong enough to move the nut.

STALKING

A lot of what needs to be said about stalking has already been covered in dealing with the art of stalking oneself, but in stalking others there are a few more points to be considered. Firstly, it should be realised that the only justification for stalking others is to receive their co-operation. No true warrior who walks the Path of Freedom will ever use stalking to force another being into doing his bidding. Never! A warrior uses stalking in order to gain a necessary advantage, but it is an act of abuse to use such an advantage for selfish gain. For example, before a surgeon performs an operation he will first need to anaesthetise his patient; but the surgeon who takes advantage of a patient whom he has anaesthetised has abused his position and is not worthy of the name. This is true also of stalking. The warrior who has mastered the art of stalking does not use it for taking unfair advantage of people.

A warrior will use stalking for two reasons; firstly, in order to stop another person from trying to manipulate him, in which case it is self-defence, and secondly, in order to help a person who might otherwise not have been able to see that he needs help. However, it must never be forgotten that warriors do not unilaterally decide who needs to be helped because this, as has already been explained, would be interfering in another person's destiny. The examples of Leon and Lydia prove this point quite well. Leon did not decide that his neighbour needed help, but because the neighbour tossed his rubbish into Leon's garden he was forced to act. The same is true about Lydia, because Lydia's actions were prompted by her sister, rather than Lydia having imposed her will upon her sister. In both of these examples the interaction of life is clearly demonstrated.

In order to stalk another person the stalker must be fully alert and completely objective, as in not-doing. It is impossible to stalk anyone when one is caught up in the situation at hand. A stalker always has the upper hand because, firstly, he is always detached from the situation, and secondly, being in full control of his emotions he can swing the situation whichever way he chooses. This is the stalker's advantage, because he can always manipulate his opponent into some form of mental state in which an emotional response will be triggered. Once a response has been triggered the stalker only has to guide his opponent in the direction he wishes him to go.

The art of stalking is nothing more than acting. However, if the stalker is going to be successful he obviously cannot let his opponent know that he is stalking him. Therefore, the stalker will often adopt a very conspicuous role which is easily recognised, but which at the same time hides his real motives. Such a conspicuous role enables the stalker to devise a plan of action, and if his opponent is unknown to him, it buys him the needed time in which to study his opponent first. To understand this more fully let us, as usual, look at an example.

Paul has been invited to dinner by friends of his. When he arrives he finds that the party is rather strained due to an uninvited guest named Mark. Mark is bent on dominating the conversation by ceaselessly trying to enforce his spiritual beliefs upon everyone present. After he is introduced to Mark, Paul sits back quietly to observe the situation, and within minutes has seen Mark for what he really is. From that moment on Paul gives Mark his undivided attention, and Mark, delighted that Paul should be so very interested in his conversation, promptly begins to convert Paul to his faith.

Paul appears to be utterly fascinated and listens with complete concentration. Occasionally he will interrupt Mark to ask for more detail on a statement Mark has just made and, without realising that he is being stalked, Mark happily expounds on his previous statement. What Paul is in effect doing is giving Mark enough rope with which to hang himself, and when Paul finally feels that he has given Mark enough rope, he begins to pull strongly on the other end. The conversation could have gone something like the following.

Mark had been talking about the importance of knowing that one's soul is saved, which prompted Paul to ask if Mark could explain what that meant. Mark obliged by launching into a full description of what happens after death and the benefits of going to heaven rather than hell. Paul then asked if it was possible for all men to go to heaven, and Mark answered that, strictly speaking, and according to the Bible, only those few who have been chosen by God can go to heaven. Paul further enquired if Mark thought that anyone in the room was possibly amongst the chosen few. At this point Mark hesitated, then answered that although it was not for him to say, it was nevertheless every man's duty to live like a good Christian. Paul then asked if only Christians could be chosen for salvation, and Mark did not hesitate to say that this was true.

At this point Paul digressed slightly and invited Mark to tell him what Christ had really taught. Mark was by now totally in his element, and told everyone in the room about the carpenter from Nazareth who taught people that they should love each other as they love themselves. To this Paul added that Christ also taught us not to judge another unless we ourselves be judged. Mark agreed with this most heartily and, in doing so, put the noose around his own neck.

Paul just looked Mark straight in the eyes and asked him why he was then trying to convert everyone in the room to Christianity. Before Mark could answer, Paul pointed out two important facts. Firstly, if only those few who have been chosen by God can go to heaven, it is a brutal lie to promise people salvation without knowing if they will be acceptable to God. Secondly, if Mark agrees that one should not judge another, he has no right to infer that those present in the room are not good Christians, or even for that matter, that they are not amongst the chosen few.

Mark hanged himself with his own words and, although Paul did not attack Mark's faith, he nevertheless put Mark firmly in his place. In other words, Paul did not harm Mark in any way, but neither did he allow Mark to hurt him or anyone else in the room. Moreover, Mark now had something to think about and learned to look a little deeper into his own religion. Admittedly, Mark was cowed and embarrassed by Paul's countermoves, but through his actions Paul helped him to see the futility of trying to enforce one's own ideas on someone else. Such is the signature of the true stalker.

Although both stalking and not-doing are complex arts which can only be mastered after a great deal of practice, if the preliminary teachings imparted here are studied and applied, they are sufficient to give the reader a broad foundation in both arts. However, there is one final issue which now warrants further explanation, namely *detachment*. This could be mentioned only very briefly at the beginning of this section.

Detachment, in the true sense of the word, is not possible unless we treat those with whom we come into contact as *mirrors* of ourselves. It is vital to remember that we cannot perceive anything which is not within our own frame of reference. Therefore, when we perceive something in another person, we must acknowledge the fact that we can only perceive it because we too possess what we have perceived. This is what is meant by using other people as our mirrors. When we do this, not only do we gain objectivity, but we are also able to keep our emotions under control.

In using other people as our mirrors we must not fall into the trap of looking only at the face value of the person's actions. It is necessary to look for the bottom line or the underlying cause. Sometimes it will be the face value of a person's actions which applies to ourselves, but at many other times it will instead be the underlying cause. Therefore, if we meet a person who is dogmatic, we should look into our own lives to find the areas in which we too are dogmatic. Likewise, if we meet a person whom we find to be especially gentle, we should look for that same gentleness in our own lives. In this respect it should be realised that mirrors can be both positive as well as negative. Let us clarify this with two examples.

Mary meets a woman whom she perceives as being

extremely arrogant. The woman manifests her arrogance by implying continuously that she is the best mother in the world and that it is thanks to her wisdom and expert guidance that all her children are so marvellous. Looking at the face value of the woman's actions, Mary comes to the conclusion that she is not at all like the woman. In fact, Mary does not even regard herself as being a particularly good mother. However, reflecting deeper upon the arrogance which the woman has mirrored for her, Mary comes to realise that she too is arrogant, but that she manifests it quite differently.

In Mary's case, she always feels that it is her duty to remain silent whenever confronted by arrogant people, mainly because she believes herself to be above such behaviour. Herein lies Mary's arrogance. By believing herself to be superior to those who are arrogant Mary smugly indulges in her aloofness.

Ben has a brother who is a brilliant scholar, but because Ben was never particularly outstanding in scholastic achievements he grew up in his brother's shadow. This never really bothered Ben, because in a way he was always very proud of his brother and often admired his brother's academic brilliance. Ben's brother went from strength to strength and in time qualified as a truly outstanding research physicist.

Ben, on the other hand, attended a trade college and after he qualified as a fitter and turner, joined a large engineering company in this capacity. However, he soon proved himself to be excellent at his job. Having recognised Ben as being above average, his supervisor encouraged him to further his trade qualifications. Ben heeded the advice, and five years later was promoted to senior designer in the company's research division.

Both Ben and his brother turned out to be equally brilliant in the field of research, Ben in engineering, his brother in physics. The brothers manifested their mutual talent differently, but the bottom line was the same.

By using people as our mirrors we learn an enormous amount about ourselves, simply because of the objectivity. As we have already discovered, it is always so much easier to see virtues and vices in other people than to see them in ourselves. Furthermore, when we know that the action of another person is merely the reflection of an aspect of ourselves, then no matter how unpleasant that action may be, it is not so easy to point a finger and become indignant. Perhaps you can say that you are not a common thief, and perhaps you will be right. But are you then an uncommon thief? How do you steal, and from whom? Do you steal time at work, or perhaps office stationery? Or do you steal from people in other, more subtle, ways?

In the final analysis a good stalker is good simply because he can and does use people as his mirrors. It is not very difficult to anticipate a man's actions or his reactions when we use ourselves as a guide. When we see people as mirrors of ourselves they all stand revealed like open books; we need only look within ourselves and all the answers are there.

CHAPTER TEN

A FINAL WORD

It will be observed that the *art of dreaming* has not been included in this volume. The reason for this is that Toltec dreaming is complex and as such lies beyond the scope of this first volume. The four practical techniques given in this book, namely, *working with emotion and intent*, *recapitulation*, *stalking* and *not-doing*, all start off in normal awareness. In dreaming, on the other hand, the apprentice already starts off in an altered state of awareness, and therefore it is not possible to include dreaming in this book, which has been written primarily from the angle of normal awareness.

At this juncture I feel that it is appropriate for me to offer a word of friendly advice. In this day and age, in which there are so many well-meaning people who are genuinely searching for the truth, drug abuse has become a serious problem. In their attempts to achieve altered states of perception and hoping thereby to gain a glimmer of knowledge, people of all ages have allowed themselves to be conned into taking trips.

As is clear from this book, there was a time when Toltecs too walked the path of drugs in desperation. Thus we do not stand in judgement of those who still walk this sad path, but from personal experience all true Toltecs will agree that in the end the results do not justify the ill-effects of drug abuse. Anyone who wishes to have real knowledge must become a whole person and must have all of his faculties fully operative. However, the damage done by drugs both to the brain and the nervous system of the physical body is irreparable, and this renders the person concerned unfit for warriorship. Once the brain or the nervous system has been damaged, full control of the emotions, and therefore of *intent*, is impossible.

Furthermore, the teachings, as well as the practical techniques given in this book, are far more powerful than they appear to be at a casual glance. Yet if the teachings are adhered to strictly, they are also perfectly safe and will lead the serious student through a steady but natural unfolding of awareness. By taking the needed time and by making the necessary effort, the student will ultimately be guided into altered states of perception, and hence to knowledge and to freedom.

However, it is the fool who will attempt to augment these teachings by using drugs simultaneously or even intermittently. Anyone foolish enough to do this will have to take responsibility for his stubbornness squarely upon his own shoulders. Psychosis engendered by a too rapid shifting of the assemblage point, or schizophrenia brought about by an assemblage point which has been permanently destabilized, is today still beyond the scope of medical science. Anyone who attempts to use drugs in conjunction with this book will force his development in an unnatural and dangerous manner and will undoubtedly risk spending the rest of his life in a mental institution!

Beware of anyone who tries to convince you otherwise. Usually such a person is not really interested in true knowledge, but has only climbed onto the bandwagon for the ride. There are those who profess to seek knowledge and freedom, but who secretly desire only the excitement of doing something different or the thrill of being anti-establishment. Then there are also those who are not interested in anything else other than feathering their own nests, and it is types such as these who will push drugs for as long as there are those suckers who fall into the trap.

Social conditioning takes a heavy toll on us all, and therefore most young people either fear being different to their friends or else just loathe being called a wimp or a nerd or such like. In this you must make up your own mind. Do you want to be a warrior, or do you prefer to bury yourself in your social conditioning and sink into the mire of mediocrity? The warrior does not fear to stand alone in his decisions, for he is a free being who carries the responsibility of his life proudly. Even if a warrior is singled out from his fellow men he can never feel victimised, because he knows the honour of living as an impeccable warrior. The real nerds of this life are those who insist upon being just like everyone else.

There is another point mentioned very briefly in the introduction to this book which warrants some more consideration and concerns the great many spiritual teachers and teachings available today. The words I am going to use now are harsh, and to many it will appear as if I am taking it upon myself to criticise and to judge. Yet the time for remaining mute has passed, and in this you are called upon to exercise your better judgement. Generally, most people mean well, but there are few today who are truly qualified to lead. In the majority of cases we have the classic example of the blind leading the blind.

Beware of those who make lofty promises and stupendous claims, because no one can really do anything for another person. We can receive guidance, but each and every one of us has to walk the path by himself and stand alone in his knowledge. Even apprentices working under a *nagal* must do the work for themselves and by themselves. The *nagal* cannot take even one step on their behalf.

Be especially wary of those who promise instant success at whatever price. There is no such thing as instant success. It is possible under extraordinary circumstances to work a miracle spontaneously, but the experience fades as quickly as it occurred, and afterwards one is still none the wiser and just as helpless as before. Anyone who wishes to have true knowledge and *power* can have it, but we all have to be prepared to invest the necessary time and effort in order to achieve the desired goal. In relation to this there is also nothing wrong in a spiritual teacher demanding payment for services rendered. Although today there are still many people in the world who adhere to the belief that all spiritual teachings should be free of charge, it should be remembered that the spiritual teacher, just like anyone else, needs to eat, pay for his electricity, rent, etcetera. However, beware of those who are very obviously taking without any apparent reinvestment.

Money is crystallized *power*, and as such is not the sole property of any one man. Money comes to us in the same way that *power* comes to us, so that we may use it and learn from it. Money, like *power*, should never be wasted, but conserved and used wisely – but it must still be used. In short, money must circulate and flow if the interrelationship of life is not to be broken. Therefore, take care that you do not divest yourself of your savings to those who are obviously only out to line their own pockets, but by the same token you must also be prepared to pay for your spiritual tuition.

In all matters spiritual and material learn to listen to your heart, because upon the path with a heart all stands clearly revealed. The rational mind may at times choose to be confused in order to avoid a thorny isssue or to conceal a hidden motive, but the heart is incapable of anything other than complete honesty. If you follow your heart you cannot con yourself, nor can anyone else pull the wool over your eyes. The mark of the true friend and the true teacher is that they uphold the interdependence, interaction and interrelationship of life. These are the people who work for unity rather than for separativeness, and who seek to love rather than to hate.

In your journey learn to distinguish with clarity between

useless information and true teachings. True knowledge and *power* can only arise out of practical experience in your daily life. If you are being victimized at work by a boss who is a petty tyrant, what good does it do you to know that there are two different races of people living on Mars? Or if you experience wonderful sensations of flight whilst in meditation, how will this help you to escape a mugger bent upon attacking you in a side-street? The true teacher who has something to offer will invariably impart teachings which can be put into practice in your daily life. It is in your daily life that you need knowledge and *power*, not in the mountains or deserts. Likewise, it is in the given moment that you will need both skill in action and *power*; therefore you will not necessarily have the time to meditate first in order to summon your *power*.

Earlier on I stated that the time for remaining mute has passed, and in this respect I have one final message. In this age of constant speculation, the truth concerning the so-called end of the world and the concepts of heaven and hell should be revealed. These concepts play upon the minds of many people, often engendering in them no small amount of fear and confusion.

At the outset, know that behind the scenes stands *The Silent Watcher, The Spirit of Atl*, surrounded by His small but powerful group of aides – They whom Toltecs have come to know and love as the *Guardians of the Race*. Unseen and unknown to humanity, these beings toil day and night, forfeiting rest and even Their own freedom so as to hold aloft the light that humanity may succeed in the great challenge with which it is faced at this time.

Atl is not the God of the Christians, nor is He Christ, or

Buddha, or Krishna, or Mahommed, or any other deity of mankind. Toltecs do not profess to know who God really is and they prefer to leave this concept to the theologians of the world. All that we can say with certainty is that Atl is not a mystical being who spends His time in listening to prayers, but a very real being whom Toltecs have come to know gradually and sequentially across a vast expanse of time. It is not for Toltecs to attempt to divulge His true identity other than to say that in the Christian Bible He is the One referred to as *'Melchizedek, the King of righteousness and of peace, who is without father, without mother, without descent, having neither beginning of days, nor end of life'*[1]. It is He Whom Toltecs refer to as the Lord of the World, the being in Whom we live and move and have our being.

In the unseen worlds Atl has unleashed mighty forces of the universe, and although humanity in general is as yet unaware of it, mankind finds itself in the midst of a battle which has already been initiated. The collapse of communism, the demolition of the Berlin Wall, the political changes in South Africa, the heavy strain upon world economics, are but a few examples of the battle being engaged. Within the next few years vast and irrevocable changes will have swept the planet. Man will either move with these mighty currents or be swept under – the choice is his. It is man's destiny to have knowledge and to wield *power*, but there is no way in which to aquire *power* other than to claim it. It is for this reason that Atl has engaged mankind in this battle – this is His *gift of power* to humanity, but man will have to claim his gift.

Toltecs are in service to The Spirit of Atl and His aides, and at this momentous time in the history of humanity we stand ready to play our part in whatever way may be necessary. This is humanity's *hour of power*, a challenge which man must face alone and unaided if his gift is not to be diminished or destroyed. Accordingly, Atl is purposefully standing back, and has forbidden even the Guardians of the Race to help or to interfere. However, because we are members of the human race, Toltecs, together with all other men and women of goodwill, have been given free rein to assist wherever possible.

The battle mentioned above concerns the so-called end of the world, but not in the sense in which this concept is normally understood. There must and will come an end to this human madness which is not only destroying man and the creatures that share the planet with him, but also destroying the planet itself. The end of the world does not imply the end of life upon earth, or for that matter the destruction of the planet. It means that the world of separativeness and destruction must and will come to an end. That awareness which is causing so much hatred, so much separativeness and so much destruction must give way to an understanding and acceptance of the interrelationship of all life and the importance of the unit to the well-being of the whole.

Is there a heaven and a hell? In a manner of speaking there is indeed both heaven and hell. Heaven is to reach the end of one's life having no regrets, knowing that one has lived a good, strong and impeccable life. Heaven is to have known what a marvellous privilege life is, and that one has loved and enjoyed every moment, every challenge of this stupendous gift. Heaven is to have loved the people and beings who have shared their lives with us. Heaven is to have loved this beautiful world within which all of this was made possible.

Hell is to reach the end of one's life filled with resentment, anger and bitterness. Hell is to know that one has hated the precious gift of life, and that one has trampled underfoot the opportunities one has been given to learn, to love and to rejoice. Hell is to know that it is not possible to turn back the clock and to say; 'I'm sorry. Let me try again.'

Heaven is to leave this wonderful world knowing that one could rejoice in life like a warrior, and did; hell is knowing that one could have rejoiced, but didn't.

As far as this present volume is concerned, there now remains little else to say other than to wish you well upon your journey. Know that our strength is your strength, just as your joy is our joy, for this is the meaning of the interrelationship of life. It is true that we must each walk the Path of Knowledge alone and unaided, and yet we are never truly alone.

Stand firm in your decision to move forward, and know that this is our sincere wish for you. Stand strong and free, unencumbered by the restraints of social conditioning, for in this we will support you. Stand bravely to fight your battle for *power*, and in that battle let your spirit flow free to rejoice in life. If you do this, then through the interaction of life we will be there to uphold you, for the spirit of man is one and rejoices in freedom and in *power*. Above all, remember always that although the spirit of man can be waylaid and delayed, it can never truly be defeated.

THE ONLY FAILURE IN LIFE IS THE FAILURE TO FIGHT.

CHAPTER ELEVEN
THE FULFILMENT OF PROPHECY

In a time even before time, when the orange-red sun was still young and the planet Earth was not yet born to flesh; when the heavens were still being torn asunder by the War of Spirit, and when man was as yet enveloped within the fiery mists of solar beingness, an oracle already ancient then, and known only as The Nameless One, looked out across the universe and, *seeing* what was to come, uttered this prophecy:

> At the end of time as man will come to measure time, Atl, Lord of that world called Earth, will send forth a call to all the leaders of mankind, instructing them to bring forth the fruits of their labours, for upon these fruits shall rest the future of that troubled world, planet of sorrow, beautiful dark gem of the universe destined to shine as unto its sister the bright planet of Dawn.....
>
> Upon the call having been sounded forth, the first men who step forward to display their wares are forceful men who bring forth a great abundance of fruits that dazzle the eye and cause the mouth to water. But as these fruits are brought to bear upon the scales of justice, a great and terrible darkness descends over all the earth, for these fruits were conceived within the dark recesses of the human mind.
>
> Atl, Lord of the World, passes no comment: only a silence reigns within the darkness. Time passes, and although the fruits harvested by the leaders of mankind are in great

abundance, yet men starve on every hand, faces contorted with the bitterness of the fruit, eyes glazed over with the hopelessness of despair.

When the great and terrible darkness has become like unto the night, and when yet more leaders step forward to offer fruit of dread and death, then from out of the darkened valleys of the land emerge a few men to address the Lord of the World.

'Lord,' they speak in unison, 'We are travellers who come from the valleys in the East, the West, the North and the South. We are but seven small bands, the Lions, the Elephants, the Tigers, the Bears, the Foxes, the Wolves and the Dragons. We come empty-handed, O Lord, for we have naught to offer other than ourselves. But in our many travels we have seen the sacred Fount of Life, to drink from which is never again to want for nourishment. If it pleases thee, O Lord, we will lead the people there, for here they will all starve to death.'

'Do as you deem wise,' answers the Lord of the World. Bowing in silent acknowledgement, the men turn to face the world with open hand and open heart. Then, beckoning all to follow, they turn to show the way, to set the pace. Some of the people follow immediately without a word: some hesitate, confused: some grumble in discontent: some openly resist, and sit down to remain and starve.

Memory! What would it be like without restoration of my memory? Peace! There would be the blissful peace born of ignorance. Ignorance versus peace! How ironic can it be? No, fool! No time now for cowardly thoughts! Remember that peace must be found anew every lifetime within the midst of the battle!

Yes! Once again, like so many times before, I must find the peace – that serene peace at the centre of the battle. Yet, for now there is still only memory – sweet, agonising memory – a memory which horrifies me, and yet a memory I would not sacrifice for the sake of a coward's sense of peace.

So once again does the history of now, the history of before now, and the history of the time before time, stalk my mind. All those people. So many hopes and dreams. So many battles won and so many lost. And the ancient prophecies. Those too do I remember – the ones that have already materialised, the ones which pertain to now, and those still suspended within the future. Still the great wheel spins out the pattern of destiny from age to age, from lifetime to lifetime. Cursed prophecies! Perhaps ignorance would be better. But then again, maybe not. What difference does it make anyway? The wheel is the wheel, and the pattern is the pattern. Still, I cannot shake off the fear of memory, the fear of all the struggle, the pain. So much pain. Always so much pain.

Atl, I do not expect you to hear, or even to listen to this; but for my own selfish sake I must ask, like I have done so many times before. Why all the fear and pain?

I see the pattern of destiny as the great wheel spins out the weave, and I understand why you took it upon yourself to make this choice. But, Atl, will it ever end?

Are we then such fools that the fear must continually be so intense, the pain so numbing? Will it truly change this time round?

How long have we laboured at this impossible task of yours, of ours? I do not mean to complain, and regrets I cannot possibly have, for you know as well as I that if we were to start anew, then again we all would willingly embark upon this same path with the same determination as before. We are you, Atl.

Your will is our duty, and your life is our honour: how can this ever be otherwise?

But, Atl, please, this time round, let it change. This time round, let us truly beat back the fear and the pain!

I will play my part, Atl, as will my brothers, and together we will fight again this endless battle. Only this time, please, let our struggle make a difference!

I only hope they will listen to us. Will they? Why should they listen to a bunch of crackpots? Yes, that is what we are, crackpots! Only madmen try to teach people what they mostly do not want to hear!

Looking down the tunnel of time I see a destiny which rings as true as the hammer upon the anvil – a struggle to mould that which resists moulding, that which must be burned white-hot in the furnace of life before it can be beaten into shape – a burning which sears the soul, a beating which stuns the mind and wounds the heart made tender by what is perhaps a naïve longing to be loved by all. Is there no end?

Atl, must this be?

.... I suppose it must!

Stupid question really; for, after all, you are the Divine Rebel, He who just had to take it upon Himself to be the Great Sacrifice! You just had to be a bloody hero, didn't you, Atl?

Damn you, I understand! But damn you for getting me into this mess! And damn all the Guardians including that fool Christ who keeps me on his leash! I'm not as strong as any of you, you know!

.... Or am I stronger than I am willing to believe?

Strong or not, can I turn away from a destiny which is me? Can I escape you, Atl? Do I even want to?

No! Damn it all! I cannot turn away from my destiny! Nor

can I stop loving you!

But why? Only tell me why there has to be so much fear? So much pain? Always so much pain!

.... They already now come to me, Atl – with their fears and their hopes.

They look at me with eyes filled with the unspoken hope of those who believe I will make it better – that I can take away the fear, the pain.

Damn you, Atl! How can I take away their fear or their pain when that fear and pain is the very essence of your own being, of our being?

How? How must I do it?

Oh yes, I know! I am who I am, and I do what I must do. But why must there always be so much fear? So much pain?

I know. Wolf I am, bringer of hope and freedom.

Not *the* hope, but *a* hope ....

.... not *the* freedom, but *a* freedom.

I know too that Dragon was I born, bringer of the two-edged sword. A sword which must cleave and divide so that the wisdom of discrimination can bring about a new unity.

.... Not *the* division, but *a* division ....

.... not *the* wisdom, but *a* wisdom.

You see, Atl, I do know! And I am willing! I am willing to stand, for I under-stand your purpose. All of those who come to me I will lead to freedom if I can. But must there be so much pain?

I am more than willing to fight, because your purpose is both my duty and my honour, for I cannot help but to love them and you. But must there be so much fear?

Stupid question once again; for I already know there is no other way!

They tell me Théun is my name – Théun Mares – and that

in the old tongue this means Théun of the Great Waters, beloved son of Mara, the One of Tears. Tears. Yes, tears. Always so many tears!

A name of old, spun out in a time I care not to remember. A name! What a laugh! I know who I am and, besides, I already have a name, a perfectly good one given to me by my parents in this lifetime. But the wheel has spun out Théun, and who can argue with the pattern? So then Théun it shall be.

Do I believe all this? Do I even *want* to believe all this? Do I have a choice? Fool! Idiot man! A warrior *has* to believe, remember? Otherwise there is nothing!

Nothing? No wheel? No pattern? No destiny?

.... No names at all! No duty! No responsibility!

Tempting that! Very tempting! But can I really accept that there is nothing except this human madness within a chaotic universe which serves no purpose?

No! Of course not! I can't! Was there ever a time I could? No! Of course not! Fool! A mad, crazy fool is what I am!

.... But ...... Atl? I know that you do understand.

Once in a while it is a great help to put destiny aside just for a little while – just for a few stolen moments of selfish desire.

But even so, I stand. I fight! How can I not?

For Wolf I am –

.... hope and freedom.

For Dragon was I born –

.... division and wisdom.

Dragon Wolf –

.... division the hope ....

.... hope the freedom ....

.... freedom the wisdom ....

Great Spirit of Atl, I, the Dragon Wolf, Théun of the Great Waters, son of Mara, the One of Tears, salute you!

I stand, and, standing thus, the Spear of Destiny flies true. I fight, and, fighting thus, the Sword of Power rings with the One Truth and flashes forth the blue flame of the One Power. I am who I am. I do what I have to do.

Atl, Lord of my being. My duty is my honour! My life is yours! This I swear upon the Rose; upon the sacred Fount of Life; and upon my spirit. For now and ever more!

Let those who have the ears to hear, hear then the ancient words of The Nameless One. Listen, as we all have listened, and learn, as we all have learned.

> You who come seeking to tread the Warrior's Path, see to it that you heed my words with care, for when I look down the tunnel of time I see that it will be a long, long while before you will grasp the deeper implications of my words. Realise too that I can but only hold out for you a vision of that which is beyond words. The Unspeakable can never be verbalised: we can only verbalise our vision of the Unspeakable. This is the Law.
>
> All of us come to the Warrior's Path in ignorance. All of us must learn that we do not know what true learning is until we walk the Warrior's Path. This is so because this path is in truth a journey into the unknown, but there is no way to know the unknown beforehand. This is the Law. Warriors are pioneers, and although the pioneers may come back to tell you of what they have discovered, such information will be mere theory to the listener, not knowledge gained from own experience. Furthermore, how will the pioneers tell you of those things they have discovered within the unknown when you can only grasp that which is the known?
>
> Therefore, if you truly wish to know what is entailed in treading the Warrior's Path, then you must tread this path

yourself: only then will your perception coincide with the vision. This is the Law. But know this much, and listen with care, for I now speak of things past, present and future: I speak of man atavistic, of hu-man, and of man conscious.

Warriors are first and foremost men, humble men, who cannot avoid the confines of the Law. Their task in life is to learn by means of mapping the great unknown. To map the unknown requires having to enter that mysterious vastness, but each time we enter into it we transmute those energy fields within us which correspond with the great unknown outside of us. This transmutation affects our entire existence, so that our very state of beingness becomes irrevocably altered. With the effects of transmutation comes eventual transformation, the emission of all that is undesirable. The inevitable product of transformation is transfiguration, a complete metamorphosis.

Know then that once this process has been initiated a chain reaction takes place which cannot be stopped. The Warrior's Path is thus a path of no return – a path of transmutation, transformation, transfiguration. This is the Law.

Go now to the task which has been assigned to you, for the time of change is upon us all! But as new recruits, Atl'aman, carry also within your hearts these words.....

This revolution of the wheel is even now closing in upon its own beginning – the serpent of wisdom shall bite its own tail! Destiny decrees that this day be ended and that this world shall become to you only a vague memory. At the close of this day you shall be transported to what shall be your new home, your new responsibility, and you shall forget all! Yet, you must struggle to remember what it is to be the warriors of Atl, what it is to be Atl'aman! And above all you must struggle to remember what it is to be Toltec! The sacred trust invested in you can never and must never be forgotten!

To this end a seed has been placed in the hearts of you all. Seven groups you are – seven seeds for seven groups.

Therefore seven times seven shall you be from now until the end of time. In this way at least some of you from each group will remember what it is to be Toltec, and that from the seven seeds must be grown the seven keys which will unlock again the seven seals of the One Power. Should you never remember this, the nagal of us all will stand bereft of the One Power and thus will be lost for ever in the ancient Darkness..... Beyond this moment I will not speak to you again, for the pattern decrees that now the fires of the forge be fanned, entered and endured.....

Warriors of Atl, I salute you!
By the love which is the essence of your own true inner fiery being!
By the impeccability which constitutes your invincible power!
By the humility which is the mark of your free spirit!
May the peace and the harmony of the Yellow Rose of Friendship abide with you now and for ever more!

Farewell, Atl'aman! Go now and learn what it is to be hu-man. Go learn what it is to stand! Go learn what it is to fight! The wheel will spin, and many times over will the great serpent bite its own tail before you will remember. But once you have begun to remember then let the Spear of Destiny fly true. Let the Sword of Power ring with the One Truth and flash forth the blue flame of the One Power!
Atl'aman! I charge you! Remember the sacred trust!
.............Remember.................
.......................remember......................

LIONHEART PUBLISHING

Visit our website for regular articles on the Warrior's Path containing insights into how the Toltec Teachings apply to everyday life situations.

www.lionheartpublishing.com

You will also find links to other sites offering valuable information and learning experiences. Our website also contains information about how to order our books throughout the world. Alternatively, contact us directly:

Lionheart Publishing
Private Bag X5
Constantia 7848
Cape Town
South Africa
e-mail: cajmi@iafrica.com
www.lionheartpublishing.com

ADDITIONAL INFORMATION

As part of his ongoing efforts to impart the Toltec Teachings to humanity, Théun, together with his Man of Action, Russell Braithwaite, runs residential programmes twice yearly in England and the United States, elucidating the deeper meanings of the teachings which are not easily explainable in writing. For further information, visit **www.warriorskeep.com**

For information about organisations separate from, but working under the guidance of Théun, visit the website below:
www.toltec-foundation.org

For your protection, and so as to avoid a possible misrepresentation and/or misinterpretation of the Toltec teachings, please be informed that none of the e-mail groups, internet discussion forums, or any other groups working in the name of Théun Mares are official representatives of Théun's work. These groups are set up independently of Hunters' Lodge, and their function is to act as a support mechanism for those who are working with Théun's teachings. The only authority on the content of Théun's work is Russell Braithwaite, Théun's Man of Action, operating from Hunters' Lodge, South Africa. *Théun has not appointed, nor does he recognise any other representative.* If he does so, details will be posted on his website.

Hunters' Lodge is the official residence of Théun Mares and the centre from which he and Russell Braithwaite, his Man of Action, conduct their activities.

- **Winds of Africa** is a South African close corporation through which Théun and Russell direct those of their activities related to the residential programmes.
- **Warriorskeep.org** and **Warriorskeep.com** are Théun's personal websites.

BIBLIOGRAPHY

CHAPTER 1

1. Helena Petrovna Blavatsky, *Isis Unveiled*, The Theosophical Publishing House, Wheaton, IL, 1994, Volume 1, p.557.

CHAPTER 2

1. Henry David Thoreau, *Dictionary of Quotations* (Oxford University Press), London, Chancellor Press, 1985, p.547 q.3. *A Week on the Concord and Merrimack Rivers, Wednesday.*
2. Johann Wolfgang von Goethe, ib.p.223 q.21 *Faust.*
3. Johann Wolfgang von Goethe, ib. p.223 q.19 *Faust.*
4. Ralph Waldo Emerson, ib. p.201 q.18 *Society and Solitude, Success.*
5. Ralph Waldo Emerson, ib. p.200 q.28 *Essays, New England Reformers.*
6. William Blake, ib. p.73 q.18 *Auguries of Innocence.*
7. Oscar Wilde, ib. p.569 q.20 *The Importance of Being Earnest.*
8. Jonathan Swift, ib. p.520 q.1 *Letter to a Young Clergyman.*
9. Stephen Spender, ib. p.509 qq.1, 2 *The Truly Great.*
10. Bernard Shaw, ib. p.490 q.35 *Man & Superman.*
11. Bernard Shaw, ib. p.490 q.34 *Man & Superman.*

12. Bernard Shaw, ib. p.489 q.11 *Antony and Cleopatra.*
13. Blaise Pascal, ib. p.374 q.4 *Pensées.*
14. Ralph Waldo Emerson, ib. p.201 q.14 *Society and Solitude, Books.*
15. Ralph Waldo Emerson, ib. p.200 q.5 *Essays.*
16. William Blake, ib. p.74 q.27 *Gnomic Verses.*
17. Walt Whitman, ib. p.567 q.21 *Song of Myself.*
18. Oscar Wilde, ib. p.569 q.31 *The Critic as Artist.*
19. Bible (King James Version), Cape Town, Bible Society of South Africa, 1988, Matthew 15:11.
20. Oscar Wilde, *Dictionary of Quotations* (Oxford University Press), London, Chancellor Press, 1985, p.570 q.12 *Soul of Man Under Socialism.*
21. William Makepeace Thackeray, ib. p.542 q.9 *Esmond.*
22. Johann Wolfgang von Goethe, ib. p.224 q.4 *Tasso.*
23. Oscar Wilde, ib. p.569 q.37 *Lady Windermere's Fan.*
24. Johann Wolfgang von Goethe, ib. p.223 q.23 *Der Gross-Cophta.*
25. Bernard Shaw, ib. p.489 q.5 *The Apple Cart.*
26. Edgar Allan Poe, ib. p.380 q.16 *A Dream within a Dream.*
27. William Shakespeare, ib. p.480 q.8 *The Tempest.*
28. Frank Herbert, *Dune Messiah*, London, NEL Books, 1981, p.107.
29. Frank Herbert, ib. p.10.
30. Herman Hesse, *Siddhartha*, London, Picador, (Pan Books Ltd.), 1991, p.113.

CHAPTER 6

1. Walter de la Mare, The Listeners, New York, W.W. Norton & Co., Inc., *The Norton Anthology of Poetry*, p.906.
2. Thomas Stearns Eliot, ib. p.1012 *Journey of the Magi*.

CHAPTER 10

1. Bible (King James Version), Cape Town, Bible Society of South Africa, 1988, Hebrews 7:2.

[illegible]

[illegible] for permission [illegible] published [illegible].

[illegible] for permission to reprint [illegible]

[illegible] for permission to reprint [illegible] (1927).

[illegible] for permission to reprint extracts from "Man and Superman" [illegible]

Faber and Faber Ltd, for permission to reprint the extracts from "Journey of the Magi" [illegible] "Collected Poems 1909–1962" published by Faber and Faber Ltd.

Harcourt, Brace & World, Inc., for permission to reprint the extract from "Journey of the Magi" in T. S. Eliot's "Collected Poems 1909–1962", copyright 1936 by Harcourt, Brace & World, Inc.; copyright © 1963, 1964 by T. S. Eliot.

Faber and Faber Ltd, for permission to reprint the extracts from "The Truly Great" [illegible] Stephen Spender's "Collected Poems 1928–1953" published by Faber and Faber Ltd.

Random House, Inc. for permission to reprint the extracts from "The Truly Great" by Stephen Spender from "Selected Poems" by Stephen Spender. Copyright © 1934 and renewed 1962 by Stephen Spender.

Peter Owen Ltd, London, for permission to reprint the extract from "Siddhartha" by Hermann Hesse.

COPYRIGHT PERMISSIONS

Grateful acknowledgement is made to the following for permission to reprint previously published material:

The Theosophical Publishing House, Wheaton, IL: for permission to reprint the extract from "Isis Unveiled", by H. P. Blavatsky.

The Literary Trustees of Walter de la Mare, and The Society of Authors as their representative: for permission to reprint " The Listeners" by Walter de la Mare. "The Complete Poems of Walter de la Mare" 1969 (USA: 1970).

The Society of Authors on behalf of the Bernard Shaw Estate: for permission to reprint extracts from "Man & Superman", "Antony and Cleopatra" and "The Apple Cart".

Faber and Faber: for permission to reprint the extract from "Journey of the Magi". T. S. Eliot – "Collected Poems 1909 – 1962", published by Faber and Faber Ltd.

Harcourt Brace & Company: for permission to reprint the extract from "Journey of the Magi". T. S. Eliot – "Collected Poems 1909 – 1962". Copyright 1936 by Harcourt Brace & Company, copyright © 1964, 1963 by T. S. Eliot.

Faber and Faber: for permission to reprint the extracts from "The Truly Great" by Stephen Spender. Stephen Spender – "Collected Poems 1928 – 1985", published by Faber and Faber Ltd.

Random House Inc: for permission to reprint the extracts from "The Truly Great" by Stephen Spender. From "Selected Poems" by Stephen Spender. Copyright © 1934 and renewed 1962 by Stephen Spender.

Peter Owen Ltd, London: for permission to reprint the extract from "Siddhartha" by Herman Hesse.

COPYRIGHT PERMISSIONS

Acknowledgement is made to the following for [illegible]

[illegible]

[illegible]

[illegible]

Faber and Faber for permission to reprint the extract from [illegible] by T. S. Eliot [illegible] published by Faber and Faber Ltd.

Harcourt Brace & World, Inc. for permission to reprint the extract from [illegible] Collected Poems 1909-1962, copyright [illegible] by Harcourt, Brace & World, Inc.; copyright © [illegible] by T. S. Eliot.

Faber and Faber for permission to reprint the extract from "The Truly Great" by Stephen Spender, reprinted from "Collected Poems 1928-1953" published by Faber and Faber Ltd.

Random House, Inc. for permission to reprint the extract from "The Truly Great", by Stephen Spender. From "Selected Poems" by Stephen Spender. Copyright 1934 and renewed 1962 by Stephen Spender.

Peter Owen Ltd, London for permission to reprint the extract from "Siddhartha" by Hermann Hesse.

INDEX

A

B

C

D

E

I

J

K

L

N

O

P

R

S

T

U

V

W

THE TOLTEC TEACHINGS SERIES
by THÉUN MARES

Cry of the Eagle
The Toltec Teachings – Volume Two

A deep adventure into the inner teachings of this ancient tradition, including how to stop the internal dialogue, how to handle the four natural enemies of mankind, plus detailed information on setting up a rapport between right and left-sided awareness, along with symbols for interpretation.

ISBN 0 620 21198 9 (Hardcover)

The Mists of Dragon Lore
The Toltec Teachings – Volume Three

"Dragon Lore" is shown as the process of actively taking charge of one's life and the future. The book explores the human psyche, introducing concepts such as the 21 aspects of awareness; the meaning and existence of alternative worlds; the 4 postulates of stalking and the 7 aspects of the stalker's rule.

ISBN 1 919792 01 5 (Hardcover)
ISBN 1 919792 02 3 (Paperback)

Shadows of Wolf Fire
The Toltec Teachings – Volume Four

Freedom is not just a mystical nebulous concept. True freedom needs to be fought for, and attained. In this fourth volume, Théun lifts the veils of myth as he takes the reader back to the roots of freedom buried within another time, another place.

Having gone back to the very beginning, Théun goes on to show what freedom means in the world today, and how, in practical terms, we can set about achieving it in our lives.

ISBN 1 919792 05 8 (Hardcover)
ISBN 1 919792 04 X (Paperback)

For more information visit www.lionheartpublishing.com